THE SMALL
BUSINESS
BANKRUPTCY KIT

Also Available by Robert L. Davidson, III

The Small Business Incorporation Kit
The Small Business Partnership Kit
Contracting Your Services
How to Form Your Own S Corporation

THE SMALL BUSINESS BANKRUPTCY KIT

Robert L. Davidson III

John Wiley & Sons, Inc.

New York · Chichester · Brisbane · Toronto · Singapore

Library of Congress Cataloging-in-Publication Data

Davidson, Robert L., III
    The small business bankruptcy kit / by Robert L. Davidson, III.
      p.   cm.
    Includes index.
    ISBN 0-471-57650-6 (alk. paper)—ISBN 0-471-57649-2
(pbk. : alk. paper)
    1. Bankruptcy—United States. 2. Small business—Law and
legislation—United States. 3. Corporate reorganizations—United
States. I. Title.
KF1524.3.D32 1992
346.73'078—dc20
[347.30678   92-433

Printed in the United States of America

10 9 8 7 6 5 4 3 2 1

PREFACE

The word *bankruptcy* creates fear in some minds, relief in others. While bankruptcy is not to be taken lightly, neither is it synonymous with doom and gloom. True, while bankruptcy used to be something to fear, today it can mean a *fresh start* when debts have become unbearable. In 1991, some one million fresh starts were sought through the bankruptcy route.

We have all heard of Chapter 11 bankruptcies where mighty corporations seek breathing spells to reinvigorate their bottom lines, but there are other forms of bankruptcy for the individual, the married couple, and the small business. That's what this book is all about.

Chapter 7 liquidation bankruptcy means selling assets and terminating debts. Anyone can use Chapter 7, but there are two other important forms of bankruptcy: Chapter 12 (Family-Farmer) and Chapter 13 (Wage-Earner). These are particularly interesting for the individual, the married couple, and the unincorporated small businessperson. A pay-back budget is created and followed. At the end of the three-year payout period, whatever debts are not paid back are erased—the slate is clean for a fresh start.

These pages will tell you more about these options and will give you the information you need to make a choice so that you can take the steps necessary to achieve your clean slate.

Good luck.

ROBERT L. DAVIDSON, III

ABOUT THE AUTHOR

Robert L. Davidson, III, is an attorney and publications consultant in Princeton, New Jersey, where he specializes in author-publisher contracts, small business law, and elder law.

He is author, coauthor, editor, or coeditor of 13 books, the most recent of which are *Contracting Your Services, The Small Business Partnership Kit, The Small Business Incorporation Kit,* and (coauthored with Arnold S. Goldstein) *How to Start Your Own S Corporation,* all published by John Wiley & Sons.

Mr. Davidson holds degrees of Bachelor and Master of Science in Chemical Engineering from the University of Missouri, and a Juris Doctor degree from Fordham University School of Law. He is licensed to practice law in New Jersey, is a member of the American Bar Association and the New Jersey State Bar Association, and of Tau Beta Pi (engineering), Sigma Xi (science), and Alpha Chi Sigma (chemistry) honor societies.

CONTENTS

THE SMALL
BUSINESS
BANKRUPTCY KIT

CHAPTER 1

WHAT BANKRUPTCY MEANS

WHAT IS BANKRUPTCY?

The word bankruptcy derives from *banque* (meaning bank) and *rupt* (meaning broken), or *broken bank*.

Bankruptcy procedure is not a new idea. Debtors in ancient Rome who failed to meet creditor demands faced slavery for themselves or their families, or, in more extreme situations, were cut up with body pieces distributed to their creditors. Ancient English law, out of which much of our present law grew, was somewhat less harsh. Today in the United States, there is a kinder bankruptcy that offers a fresh start to businesses and individuals overburdened by debt.

Bankruptcy law began as a method of legal traffic control between competing creditors seeking to satisfy debts by seizing the property of debtors. Elements of this ancient bankruptcy law continue today. For example, the idea of "first in time, first in sight" favors creditors who file early claims over those who are slow to react.

The early history of bankruptcy law in the United States was a confusion of enactments and repeals. Finally in 1898, Congress enacted the bankruptcy law that, with periodic amendments, evolved into today's regulations.

Bankruptcy law, as found in United States Code Title 11 and as practiced today, is the result of several revisions and amendments, the latest of which was in April 1991 when the United States Supreme Court adopted amendments that took effect on August 1, 1991, and which are reported in United States Code Title 28, Section 2075.

TYPES OF BANKRUPTCY

Before you can decide if bankruptcy is a desirable course of action for you or your business, you need to understand what the various forms of bankruptcy are and what they can or cannot do for you. Each form is tailored to resolve specific types of debtor–creditor relationships.

Liquidation Bankruptcy

Chapter 7 Liquidation is what the public generally thinks of when they hear the word *bankruptcy*. Chapter 7 can be voluntarily filed by a debtor who is insolvent, or it can be forced involuntarily onto a debtor by a creditor. This solution is often sought when debts are too burdensome for payment. Assets are sold (liquidated) by a court-appointed trustee to pay the trustee's fees and as many creditors as possible. The entire procedure is usually over within 90 days.

   If the debtor is a business, it will no longer exist at the end of the bankruptcy procedure. The business may be allowed to continue operating during bankruptcy if such operation will lead to a more orderly and satisfactory liquidation.

   If the debtor is an individual or a married couple filing Chapter 7 bankruptcy, Congress has legislated to exempt property considered essential to allow the bankrupt debtor to make a fresh start. Most states have their own fresh-start lists of property and other assets that are exempt from debt liquidation during the bankruptcy procedure. Any power or authority exercised by the debtor for the benefit of another, such as a trust for one's children, is not subject to the bankruptcy liquidation.

Reorganization Bankruptcy

Chapter 11 Reorganization is the most widely used form of bankruptcy protection relied on by business. It can be called on by both businesses and individuals who seek to avoid liquidating their assets but need temporary relief from creditor demands while they reorganize their affairs, hopefully emerging as financially viable. The Bankruptcy Court must approve the Reorganization Plan. This must be a formal, written plan appropriately prepared and submitted to the Bankruptcy Court. Chapter 11 bankruptcy may drag on for several years.

Family-Farmer Bankruptcy

Chapter 12 Family-Farmer bankruptcy combines elements of Chapter 11 Reorganization bankruptcy and Chapter 13 Wage-Earner bankruptcy. It is limited to family-owned farms or other agricultural businesses with debts no larger than $1.5 million.

   The debtor creates a pay-back plan, usually lasting for three years, meanwhile maintaining control of the operation of the farm. This plan, like the Reorganization Plan, must be a formal written plan. Any debts not completely repaid during the pay-back plan period are *discharged* by the Bankruptcy Court. A trustee is appointed to collect payments from the debtor and distribute them to the creditors, and to monitor (but not control) the operation of the farm.

Wage-Earner Bankruptcy

Chapter 13 Wage-Earner bankruptcy is designed for persons with wages or draws from their businesses where income is sufficient and stable enough to provide for regular debt payments to be made to a trustee under a court-approved plan. Secured debt is limited to $350,000, and unsecured debt is limited to $100,000. The plan normally continues for three years, but can be extended to five years with the permission of the Bankruptcy Court.

Other Bankruptcy Types

There is a so-called *Chapter 20* bankruptcy technique used to take advantage of the broad discharge provisions (discharge even of debts incurred by fraud, false financial statements, or other prohibited activities) of Chapter 13 bankruptcy. It starts with a Chapter 7 Liquidation to discharge most of the outstanding debts through liquidation, followed immediately by a Chapter 13 Wage-Earner bankruptcy to partially pay, then discharge, debts not relieved by Chapter 7. This technique is most often favored by "wheeler-dealer" types.

There are specialized bankruptcy procedures for other types of debtor businesses; discussion of these special areas is beyond the scope of this book. These include:

- Railroads.
- Insurance companies.
- Stockbrokers.
- Commodity brokers.
- Banks, savings banks, credit unions, and such.
- Municipalities (Chapter 9 bankruptcy).

WHAT BANKRUPTCY CAN DO

The primary reason for most bankruptcies, other than Chapter 11 Reorganization, is the *discharge* (court-ordered elimination or eradication) of unpaid debts. Creditors are forbidden to take any action to force payment of a debt during the bankruptcy procedures, or after the debt has been discharged by the Bankruptcy Court.

In general, the immediate benefit achieved by filing for bankruptcy is the *Automatic Stay,* a court injunction to *stay* or prohibit any actions by creditors to collect a debt without court permission. Property is protected. Liens cannot be created or enforced during the bankruptcy against property for a prebankruptcy claim.

Note, however, a lien by a *secured creditor* does survive discharge, and the secured creditor may seek payment or foreclosure after completion of the bankruptcy procedure through a *Motion to Lift Stay.* No federal tax proceeding may be begun or continued against the debtor unless requested by the debtor. Utility service must continue, despite past debts, if the debtor can provide security for future service.

If the debtor has items of property, equipment, tools, or special supplies considered essential for future financial recovery, and such items are not exempted from liquidation by federal or state statutes, the debtor may be able to save them form bankruptcy liquidation by *reaffirmation of the debt* followed by *redemption*, if an agreement can be reached with the creditor on terms of payment. In other cases, the open-market liquidation value of an item may be so small that the trustee will abandon it back to the debtor.

Chapter 7 Bankruptcy

Discharge for a liquidation bankruptcy varies, depending on the type of debtor. Individual debts are discharged, unless prohibited by the court because of certain prohibited actions by the debtor, mostly related to some form of fraud or deceit.

Corporations and partnerships, in contrast, are not discharged from their unpaid debts. After all, when all assets have been liquidated, there is little reason for discharge.

Chapter 11 Bankruptcy

As noted earlier, Reorganization bankruptcy provides court protection for a business to continue operations under a court-approved *Reorganization Plan*. The objective is to save the business; the hope is that the business will emerge from the bankruptcy as a viable, competitive entity. A breathing spell is granted for the paying of old debts. While there is no ultimate discharge of debts, there may be a request by secured creditors to foreclose on the property securing their loans.

Chapter 12 Bankruptcy

The discharge from Family-Farmer bankruptcy is similar to that obtained by individuals or married couples through Chapter 7 bankruptcy. In essence, at the end of the payment-plan period, all remaining debts are discharged, with some exceptions.

There is no discharge of a debt included in a plan where the last payment is due after the date on which the plan is completed. Also, even though Chapter 13 was the model for Chapter 12, there is no discharge for an individual's taxes, or debts induced by fraud, use of false financial statements, embezzlement, or larceny.

Chapter 13 Bankruptcy

Property controlled under Wage-Earner bankruptcy includes all personal income plus property acquired after filing for bankruptcy. Discharge for this type of bankruptcy includes a number of debts not discharged under Chapters 7, 11, or 12 bankruptcy, including:

- Individual taxes.
- Debts induced by fraud.
- Debts induced by use of a false financial statement.
- Debts induced by embezzlement or larceny.
- Debts based on a willful injury caused by the Debtor.

WHAT BANKRUPTCY DOESN'T SOLVE

Bankruptcy will not resolve all debt problems, particularly for individuals where the fact of a bankruptcy may be referred to in credit ratings for up to 10 years. Even after completion of a Chapter 7 liquidation procedure, an individual may be held liable for:

- Taxes and customs duties.
- Money, property, or services obtained through false pretenses, false representation, or actual fraud.
- Money, property, services, or credit obtained through a false financial statement.
- Alimony and child support owed to a spouse, former spouse, or child.
- Debts to creditors who were unaware of the bankruptcy proceeding and who were not listed in the debtor bankruptcy filing.
- Debts resulting from larceny, embezzlement, or defalcation while acting as a fiduciary.
- Results of willful and malicious injury to another.
- Fines, penalties, or forfeitures (other than a tax penalty) owed a government (local, state, federal).
- Educational loans guaranteed by a governmental unit.
- Judgment against debtor for operating a motor vehicle while intoxicated.

Also, certain actions against a debtor are not affected by the Automatic Stay and are allowed by the Bankruptcy Code. In general, these are not financial actions, rather they are those that concern the public good. For example, the Automatic Stay does not prohibit:

- Criminal action against the debtor.
- Collection of funds for restitution under a criminal conviction or probation not merely to collect a debt.
- Collection of alimony, maintenance, or support from property not included in the bankruptcy.
- Honoring (or refusing to honor) a check or other negotiable instrument by a bank after bankruptcy is filed.

- Landlord action to regain nonresidential property under a lease that expired prior to start of bankruptcy.

- Commencement or continuation of action by a government unit under its police or regulatory powers to enforce a judgment, such as for pollution control or regulation of sale of alcoholic beverages.

- "Set-off" of an account by a stockbroker, financial institution, or others concerning commodity, foreign, or security contracts that clear to margin or guarantee or settle commodity contracts.

- Action to execute a lien within 10 days of bankruptcy if state law so provides and the creditor transferred the property to the debtor within the allowed time period.

- Commencement of action by the Department of Housing and Urban Development (HUD) to foreclose a mortgage or deed of trust if five or more living units are involved in the foreclosure.

- Issuance of a tax deficiency by a governmental unit.

- Certain actions by the Secretary of Commerce under the Ship Mortgage Act or the Merchant Marine Act.

If a creditor violates some aspect of the Automatic Stay, the creditor may be held in *Contempt of Court*. The creditor may, however, file a *Motion to Lift Stay* with the Bankruptcy Court to seek permission to proceed in an otherwise prohibited action against the debtor.

BEFORE YOU FILE FOR BANKRUPTCY

If you are drowning under the weight of debts and are considering filing for bankruptcy, here are important considerations:

- If your debt-overburden problem rests on one or two major debt items, can you forfeit these items to repossession by the creditor to cancel the debt rather than place all your assets at risk through bankruptcy?

- Don't give up anything until you are forced to do so, even though you are in arrears in payments. Often, you and your creditors can work out a new payment plan that they will accept and that you can handle.

- Even though you are hard-pressed to make payments, *never* write a check when you don't have funds in the bank to cover it. A bad (rubber) check can be a criminal offense. It is better not to pay at all.

- If you do anticipate filing for bankruptcy, don't try to hide your property or other assets by transferring them to a friend or family member. At the very least, if it is too close to the time of your filing, the trustee appointed by the Bankruptcy Court will find it and bring it back into your *Bankruptcy Estate* for the mutual benefit of all of your creditors. At worst, you may find yourself accused of fraud, and any benefit you gained through the act of bankruptcy can be canceled.

- Avoid making *preferential payments* to a favorite vendor just before filing for bankruptcy. As before, if it is too close to the time of your filing, the trustee will cancel the payment and bring it back into your *Bankruptcy Estate* for the benefit of all your creditors.
- Don't think that you can embark on a sudden wild credit card spending spree just before filing bankruptcy. Your new debts will not be shielded by the Bankruptcy Court.

CHAPTER 2

GETTING STARTED

THE IMPORTANCE OF GOOD ADVICE

The Debtor's Attorney

Bankruptcy is not a game, like Monopoly, but is a highly specialized area. Not every attorney is prepared to handle a bankruptcy petition. Some states recognize bankruptcy as a legal specialty, certifying attorneys who pass a test and can show a certain minimum amount of experience working with bankruptcy.

Larger law firms tend to conduct their bankruptcy practice with banks and financial institutions. To avoid the possibility of conflict of interest they often refuse to represent debtors. As a consequence, debtors often look to small law firms or sole practitioners who specialize in representing debtors.

Finding a Lawyer

How does the debtor find a lawyer to handle his or her bankruptcy petition? There are several sources, including:

- Lists of bankruptcy specialists from state bar associations.
- Recommendations from other attorneys in your location.
- Attorney directories listing areas of practice, such as Martindale-Hubble.
- Attorneys who advertise bankruptcy services.
- A call to the clerk of the nearest Bankruptcy Court (look it up in your phone directory). This source may yield the names of local bankruptcy trustees from whom you can get names of local attorneys active in bankruptcy law.

What should you look for in a bankruptcy attorney? Look first for experience in the type of bankruptcy you intend to file. The law is complex, and specialization is important. Then look for an attorney you feel comfortable with, one who understands you and your problems. Finally, find an attorney you can afford. Don't feel you must accept the first attorney you visit. Keep looking until you find the person you want.

"TERMS OF ART" GLOSSARY

The legal meanings of words and phrases often contain concepts and subtle shadings that are not immediately obvious from their general dictionary definitions. The following terms, important to an understanding of bankruptcy law, are defined according to their usages in bankruptcy proceedings. Words in italic type within definitions are defined elsewhere in this listing.

abandonment   the abandoning of a Chapter 7 bankruptcy property back to a secured creditor if the debtor has no equity in it

administrative expense claim   claims for expenses incurred after the bankruptcy is filed; includes attorneys' and accountants' fees and other costs of administering the bankruptcy on behalf of the debtor

Automatic Stay   legal mechanism to protect the bankrupt debtor and the debtor's property from debt collection during the bankruptcy; forces suspension of debt collection immediately on the filing of the bankruptcy petition

balance sheet test   test for insolvency; as long as assets exceed liabilities, the debtor is not considered insolvent

bankruptcy   the placing of the assets of a debtor under the control of a Bankruptcy Court to satisfy the rights of the creditors in their claims against the *Bankruptcy Estate*

Bankruptcy Estate   property included in the bankruptcy and controlled by the Bankruptcy Court

bankruptcy schedule   list of assets and debts filed with the Bankruptcy Court

bar date   last date on which the court will allow a new claim to be filed against a bankrupt debtor by a creditor; any claim not filed by that date is barred; that is, it is no longer a legally binding obligation if the creditor knew of the bankruptcy

blue-sky laws   laws that provide for the regulation and supervision of investment companies (such as limited partnerships) to protect the public from fraudulent investment schemes

book value   the value of company assets after deducting all liabilities

Chapter 7 bankruptcy   also known as *Liquidation bankruptcy*

Chapter 11 bankruptcy   also known as *Reorganization bankruptcy*

Chapter 12 bankruptcy   also known as *Family-Farmer bankruptcy*

Chapter 13 bankruptcy   also known as *Wage-Earner bankruptcy*

Chapter 20 bankruptcy combination of *Chapter 7* and *Chapter 13* filings

claim in bankruptcy, a creditor's demand for the right of payment or the performance of a promise by a debtor

closed case completion of a *Chapter 7* bankruptcy when the *Trustee* files a final report of distribution with the Court, accounting for all property of the *Bankruptcy Estate* and the proposed distribution of funds

closely held corporation small *corporation* with a limited number of *shareholders* and having no general market for selling corporation shares to the public

codebtor party who is liable for a debt along with the debtor for payment of the debt owned by the debtor; not protected by an *Automatic Stay*

collateral security given in addition to the direct security, and subordinate to it, as guaranty for its validity; if direct security fails, the creditor may claim the collateral security

cosigner see *codebtor*

contempt of court willful disregard or disobedience or other obstruction of the authority of the court

corporate shield protection of personal assets from business liabilities through incorporation

corporation "artificial person" created under the authority of law; normally an association of a number of persons (the *shareholders*) and surviving the resignation or death of any one of the shareholders

cram-down the Court implements a *Chapter 11* Reorganization Bankruptcy Plan by forcing acceptance of the plan by a class of resisting creditors when the Court considers the plan to be fair and equitable for that class

creditors' committee committee formed by creditors to the bankrupt debtor; has the same authority allowed to individual creditors

cross-collateralized loan requirement that the bankrupt debtor's assets obtained after the bankruptcy be used to help secure pre- and postbankruptcy loans

custodian party holding property of the debtor as custodian of the property; must cease custodial operations as soon as bankruptcy is known

Debtor-in-Possession in *Chapter 11* bankruptcy, the bankrupt debtors perform as their own *trustee* with all the powers and authority of a trustee in any other type of bankruptcy; also known as *DIP*

defalcation misuse of funds; e.g., embezzlement

default failure to take a required action or legal duty

deposition testimony of a witness taken under oath in response to interrogatories (questions) and converted to writing for use during court proceedings

DIP see *Debtor-in-Possession*

discharge of debts elimination or eradication of a debt by the Bankruptcy Court

disclosure statement   statement of the financial condition of the debtor and why the debtor filed bankruptcy

domicile   true, fixed, and permanent home and principal establishment

equity   ownership investment in property

exempt property   property in the bankrupt debtor's estate that is exempted from the bankruptcy as necessary for a fresh start; available only for individuals or married couples; in *Chapter 7* bankruptcy, property not exempted is subject to liquidation for payment of the debtor's debts

Family-Farmer bankruptcy   *Chapter 12* bankruptcy

fiduciary duties   duties related to the handling of finances, property, or other matters for the benefit of another party; implies a high degree of confidence and trust with good faith

for-cause extension   Court-granted permission to extend the period of payments under a bankruptcy plan

foreclosure   termination of debtor's property rights

fraud (actual)   an individual's intentional deception of a person or business granting money, property, or services at the time the grant is made

general partnership   business form in which two or more individuals or business organizations agree to operate a business together

good faith   honesty of intention

impaired creditor   creditor whose rights are hurt by a plan for *Chapter 11* Reorganization Bankruptcy

indubitable equivalent   the circumstance of the value of alternative property being clearly equivalent to the value of property in question

insider   for an individual debtor: a relation, a general partner, or relation to a general partner; for a corporate debtor: a director, officer, person in control of the debtor, a partnership in which the debtor is a general partner, a general partner of the debtor, or a relative of the general partner, director, officer, or person in control the debtor; for a partnership debtor: a general partner in or of the debtor, a partnership in which the debtor is a general partner, a relative of a general partner or person in control of the debtor, or a person in control of the debtor

insider payment   *preferential payment* to a favored relative or business associate

insolvency   individual or business unable to pay debts

Interim Trustee   court-appointed *trustee* for legal control of all property of the bankrupt debtor; serves until first meeting of creditors, at which time a permanent trustee is elected

involuntary bankruptcy   action filed by a creditor against a debtor, usually when the creditor fears that the debtor is in the process of liquidating assets and closing down the business without making provisions for payment of debts

joint and several liability a creditor's option to sue one or more or all of the parties to the liability separately or all together for the total amount of the liability

joint stock company unincorporated business association with the power and privileges of a private corporation

joint venture for bankruptcy purposes, usually treated as a partnership; meaning varies greatly from state to state

judgment culmination of a court action by declaring that the plaintiff is or is not entitled to a recovery

lease contractual agreement that gives rise to the relationship of the property owner (lessor) with the property user (lessee)

lien charge held on property for the satisfaction of a debt or duty, as in a bank holding a mortgage on property until the loan is repaid, or a contractor's lien on property for work done on the property by the contractor

limited partnership partnership where limited partners are liable for partnership business debts only to the extent of their individual contributions to or investment in the partnership

liquidation settling a debt or liability to another party by payment or other form of satisfaction; the conversion of tangible or intangible assets to money through sale

Liquidation bankruptcy see *Chapter 7* bankruptcy

matrix alphabetical list of creditors and their addresses for a bankruptcy

mortgage form of *lien*

Motion to Lift Stay motion by bankruptcy creditor to the Bankruptcy Court to allow the creditor to collect a bankrupt's debt or foreclose on a bankrupt's property despite the *Automatic Stay*; a request to modify an *Automatic Stay*

nondischargeable debt debt for bankrupt debtor that cannot be discharged (terminated) by bankruptcy action

nonexempt property property returned to the secured lienholder at the end of a *Chapter 7* bankruptcy

partnership form of unincorporated business operated jointly by two or more parties (individuals or organizations); may file for Chapter 7, 11, or 12 bankruptcy but not Chapter 13; see also *general partnership, limited partnership*

Petition for Relief request for bankruptcy protection filed with the Bankruptcy Court

preferential payments payment made preferentially by a bankrupt debtor to a creditor shortly before filing for bankruptcy; the Bankruptcy Court may order return of the payment to the debtor for the benefit of all creditors

priority claim see *priority creditor*

priority creditor creditor with a claim on the bankrupt debtor's assets with priority over the claims of other creditors

priority taxes   category of tax claims usually granted over general unsecured claims in a bankruptcy proceeding

Private Trustee   individual or corporation appointed by the Bankruptcy Court to act as *trustee* in a particular case

promissory note   promise in writing by one party to pay to another party a specified sum at a specific time or on demand

public auction   sale of property at auction where any and all persons who choose are permitted to attend and offer bids

publicly held corporation   corporation with shares traded freely on the open market, and regulated by the Securities Exchange Commission (SEC), *blue-sky laws,* and other regulations

reaffirmation of debt   bankrupt debtor's *redemption* of property that is exempted from the bankruptcy proceeding; debtor must reaffirm that the debt exists and continue to make payments owed for the property

redemption   see *reaffirmation of debt*

Reorganization bankruptcy   *Chapter 11* Bankruptcy

S corporation   election by corporation *shareholders* for a special form of corporation under Subchapter S of the tax code; profits and losses pass directly to the corporate shareholders instead of as dividends after being taxed on the corporate level

secured creditor   creditor holding a lien on a debtor's property as security for a debt; used to secure either payment or performance by the debtor

secured debt   see *secured creditor*

secured property   see *secured creditor*

shareholder   owner of a portion (share) of a corporation; ownership is represented by a share certificate or record

Standing Trustee   *trustee* appointed by the Bankruptcy Court to act as trustee for all bankruptcy cases of a particular type filed in that court

Subchapter S corporation   see *S corporation*

subrogation   substitution of one person or party for another with reference to a lawful claim, demand, or right

surety company   company whose business it is to assume the responsibility for a surety (money guarantee) for *trustees* or others with *fiduciary duties*

tax lien   *lien* held by taxing authority on the property of a debtor

341 Meeting   another name for First Meeting of Creditors in a bankruptcy proceeding

trustee   in bankruptcy, a court appointee who fulfills one of two basic roles: (1) takes possession of and liquidates the assets and business of the bankrupt debtor under the Court's supervision, and distributes the proceeds to creditors in all *Chapter 7* and *11* bankruptcies; (2) acts as a collection and disbursement agent to receive monthly payments from Debtors, disbursing them to various creditors in all *Chapter 12* and *13* bankruptcies

unimpaired creditor creditor whose rights are not harmed by a *Chapter 11* Reorganization Plan

unsecured claim see *unsecured creditor*

unsecured creditor creditor not secured by a *lien* on the property of the debtor and not otherwise in a priority category

Wage-Earner bankruptcy see *Chapter 13* Bankruptcy

CHAPTER 3

WHAT YOU NEED TO KNOW

You may have heard horror stories about what happens to you if you file for bankruptcy. True, the fact of bankruptcy may be carried in your credit report for a specified period of time. Otherwise, the Bankruptcy Code prohibits discrimination against a bankrupt business or individual.

Government agencies may not suspend, revoke, or refuse to issue licenses or permits. Private business may not discriminate against a bankrupt person or a person associated with a bankrupt person. And employers may not discriminate against an individual for not paying a debt that was discharged by bankruptcy.

If you feel that you are the victim of discrimination because of bankruptcy, protect yourself. See your lawyer.

THE TYPES OF BANKRUPTCY

Before you file for bankruptcy, it is important that you have available certain basic information for making an educated and informed decision.

The four most commonly used types of bankruptcy were discussed in Chapter 2. They are straight or *Liquidation bankruptcy* (Chapter 7), *Reorganization bankruptcy* (Chapter 11), *Family-Farmer bankruptcy* (Chapter 12), and *Wage-Earner bankruptcy* (Chapter 13). For individuals and small businesses, Chapters 7, 12, and 13 are of greatest interest. Because Chapter 11 Reorganization bankruptcy can be quite complex and costly, with extremely large attorney fees, it is usually used by large corporations with many debts and numerous creditors.

Also, as discussed in Chapter 2, there is a so-called Chapter 20 bankruptcy. The debtor first files in Chapter 7 to liquidate assets and discharge major debts, followed by Chapter 13 to take advantage of the broad areas of discharge not allowed by Chapter 7 (see Chapter 4).

Other special types of bankruptcy procedures, not discussed in this book, are designed for:

- Railroads.
- Insurance companies.
- Banks, savings banks, credit unions, and similar institutions.
- Stockbrokers.
- Commodity brokers.
- Municipalities (Chapter 9).

WHO CAN FILE BANKRUPTCY

Almost any business or individual can file for bankruptcy as long as certain requirements are met. Primarily, bankruptcies are filed by debtors unable to manage their debt loads without temporary relief (Chapters 11, 12, and 13), or so far in debt that there is little if any chance of recovery (Chapter 7). While individuals can file for Chapters 7, 12, or 13, businesses can file in any of the four types. Chapters 12 and 13, however, are limited to small businesses with limited debts.

The person or business filing for bankruptcy, called the *debtor*, must have property or legal domicile in the United States and must be a single entity (a person or married couple, a partnership, a corporation, or other type of business organization). Married couples, under bankruptcy law, are treated as a single entity. A corporation filing jointly with an individual is not protected; the individual and the corporation both must file separately for protection.

Chapter 7 and 11 bankruptcies can be voluntary (the debtor files a Petition for Relief), or involuntary (a creditor forces the debtor into bankruptcy). The usual reason for forcing an involuntary bankruptcy is that a creditor fears the debtor will liquidate assets without paying a debt, or that one creditor wants to prevent collection of a debt by another creditor. An involuntary bankruptcy against a debtor can be filed by three or more creditors if their combined unsecured claims amount to at least $5,000. If there are fewer than 12 creditors, a single creditor can force a bankruptcy. A debtor who has been forced into bankruptcy involuntarily has the right to convert the involuntary bankruptcy into a voluntary form.

Sole Proprietorships

The *sole proprietorship* is the simplest form of business—an individual doing business on his or her own behalf, legally an "extension" of the person. Income from the business is treated as individual income for federal tax purposes; losses are individual losses.

The sole proprietorship may file Chapter 7, 11, 12, or 13. For Chapters 12 and 13, there are debt limits, as discussed in Chapter 4 of this book. Chapter 11 is normally too complex and costly for a sole proprietorship, usually a small business.

Partnerships

In a *partnership*, two or more entities (that is, individuals, other partnerships, corporations, other businesses, or any combination of these) agree to operate a business together. The partnership may file for Chapter 7, 11, or 12 bankruptcy, but not Chapter 13.

All the partners must authorize filing of a bankruptcy petition by the partnership. A warning: only the partnership, not the individual partners, is protected by the filing. Individual partners, under the legal concept of *joint and several liability*, remain liable for the partnership debts. For personal protection, the individuals involved in the partnership must also file for bankruptcy.

Limited Partnerships

Limited partners, as nonmanaging investors in a partnership, have liabilities limited to the amounts they have invested in the partnership. While their potential total losses are no greater than their investments, they may wish to file for Chapter 7, 11, or 12 bankruptcy protection. Chapter 13 is not available for limited partners as such.

Corporations

A *corporation* is an "artificial person" created by law, an entity unto itself. As such it can do anything an individual can, such as sue and be sued, pay taxes, sign contracts, and more.

As an entity separate from its *shareholders*, the corporation's debts are its own, not those of the shareholder owners. The total that any shareholder can lose in a bankruptcy action is the amount the shareholder has invested in the corporation; with exceptions of certain illegal activities by shareholder/employees that will reach through the corporate shield. Chapters 7, 11, and 12 are available to corporations, but not Chapter 13.

Special corporation forms, such as *S Corporations* or *Closely Held Corporations*, are treated the same as are corporations in general.

Other Business Forms

Joint stock companies and *business trusts*, namely unincorporated associations with the powers and privileges of a private corporation, are treated as corporations for purposes of bankruptcy filing and protection, as are *joint ventures*.

THE BANKRUPTCY TRUSTEE

The type of *trustee* depends on the type of bankruptcy. In Chapter 7 Liquidation bankruptcy (and occasionally for Chapter 11 Reorganization bankruptcy), the trustee becomes the "owner" of the *Bankruptcy Estate*, liquidates it by sale or auction, and distributes the proceeds to creditors according to their priorities and classifications.

In Chapter 11 Reorganization bankruptcy, the debtor organization (called the *Debtor-in-Possession*) continues to operate the business and is, for all practical purposes, the trustee (unless some special situation develops requiring an appointed trustee). In Chapter 12 Family-Farmer bankruptcy and Chapter 13 Wage-Earner bankruptcy, the trustee's primary functions are to monitor the bankrupt debtor, collect payments from the debtor, and distribute them to the creditors, again according to priority and classification.

Trustee Characteristics

The trustee generally represents and protects the debtor's Bankruptcy Estate for the benefit of both the debtor and the debtor's creditors. The trustee:

- Can sue and be sued.
- Can be a person or a corporation.
- Must live in or have an office in or adjacent to the judicial district of the pending case (except for Chapter 11).
- Does not need to be an attorney, but is allowed to hire an attorney and other professionals as needed for the duties of trusteeship; if an attorney, may bill the Bankruptcy Estate separately for trustee duties and for attorney fees.

The trustee must post bond for faithful performance within five days of appointment. To perform necessary duties, the trustee must be notified of any motion or other Bankruptcy Court pleading filed in the case.

Types of Trustees

A *Private Trustee* is an individual or corporation appointed for a particular bankruptcy case, most often for Chapter 7 Liquidation bankruptcies.

A *Standing Trustee* is a trustee appointed by the Bankruptcy Court to handle all cases of a particular type in a particular court where there is a large volume of bankruptcies; most often for Chapter 12 or 13 bankruptcies.

The *U.S. Trustee* is found in districts where Congress has established offices of the U.S. Trustee. The U.S. Attorney General may appoint U.S. Trustees for five-year terms. The U.S. Trustee is a federal employee with a staff of accountants, economists, statisticians, and so on, as needed. This person establishes panels of Chapter 7 and Chapter 11 Private Trustees and may appoint Chapter 12 and 13 Standing Trustees. The U.S. Trustee oversees Chapter 11 Reorganization cases prior to confirmation of the Reorganization Plan.

Trustee Payment

Payment for trustee duties is based on the money distributed to creditors as follows:

Bankruptcy Action	Type of Trustee	Duties	Payment Schedule
Chapter 7	Private Trustee	Takes possession of debtor's assets, liquidates them, distributes proceeds to creditors	15% of 1st $1,000; 6% of amount between $1,000 and $3,000; 3% over $3,000
Chapter 11	Private Trustee	In cases involving fraud, mismanagement, etc., court may appoint trustee to operate the business	Same as Chapter 7
	U.S. Trustee (if appointed)	Oversees general administration of all Chapter 11 cases; acts in conjunction with private trustee, if any	Same as Chapter 7
Chapter 12	Private Trustee (if appointed)	Receives and monitors debtor's payments under the plan; disburses payments to creditors; in cases of fraud or mismanagement, court may order trustee to operate the debtor's business	Allowed 5% of funds disbursed as compensation Allowed 5% of funds disbursed as expenses; compensation cannot exceed salary of a GS-16 level federal employee
Chapter 13	Private Trustee (if appointed)	Receives and monitors debtor's payments under the plan; disburses payments to creditors	Same as Chapter 12

THE STATUS OF DEBTOR'S PROPERTY

Once bankruptcy is filed, the Bankruptcy Court controls and protects the debtor's property for the ultimate benefit of both the debtor and the debtor's creditors. Without court authorization, the debtor cannot dispose of the property and the creditors cannot repossess property in the Bankruptcy Estate. In general, the debtor's property that is eligible to become part of the Bankruptcy Estate includes:

- Inventory, equipment, or other property of the debtor.
- Debts owed by the debtor.

- Credits that may be applied to the debtor's accounting.
- Books, records, and papers of the debtor.

Debtor's Property and the Automatic Stay

The first benefit gained after filing for bankruptcy is the *Automatic Stay,* which immediately bars creditors from actively pursuing debtors for payment of debts, even before the judge of the Bankruptcy Court signs the petition. All creditor collection pressures must stop. A creditor is not even allowed to make a phone call to discuss a disputed bill. A creditor who violates the *Automatic Stay* can be punished for *contempt of court.*

While the Automatic Stay relieves the debtor of collection pressures, the primary purpose is to protect the rights of the creditors themselves. One creditor is prohibited from collecting and improving its position at the expense of other creditors. In more technical terms, the Automatic Stay prevents *preferential payments* by the debtor to a favored creditor.

What the Automatic Stay Prohibits   Once in force, the Automatic Stay provides that:

- No action may be taken against the debtor to collect, assess, or recover payment for a claim that arose before the beginning of the bankruptcy case after the bankruptcy has been filed.
- No court case (lawsuit) against the debtor may be started or continued against the debtor after the bankruptcy is filed.
- No debt collection or foreclosure act may be taken to obtain property protected by the bankruptcy; that is, repossession is prohibited.
- No judgment against the debtor may be enforced against the debtor's property that is protected by the bankruptcy.
- No administrative hearing may be started against the debtor that could have been filed prior to the bankruptcy.
- No lien may be created, perfected, or enforced against property protected by the bankruptcy, or against the debtor for a claim that arose before the bankruptcy was filed.
- No debt may be *setoff* against money due the debtor, and
- No federal tax proceeding may be begun or continued against the debtor unless requested by the debtor.

What the Automatic Stay Permits   The creditor is allowed specified actions, however, while the Automatic Stay is in force including:

- A criminal action commenced or continued against the debtor.
- Funds collected for restitution under a criminal conviction or probation, but not merely to collect a debt.

- Alimony, maintenance, or support collected from debtor's property that is not included in the bankruptcy.
- A bank's honoring of (or refusal to honor) a check or other negotiable instrument after the bankruptcy is filed.
- Landlord action to regain property under lease for nonresidential use when the lease expired prior to the commencement of the bankruptcy.
- Actions started or continued by a government unit to enforce police or regulatory powers, or enforce a judgment thereunder, such as pollution control or sale of alcoholic beverages.
- Setoff of accounts, as specified in the Bankruptcy Code, by stockbrokers, financial institutions, or others concerning commodity contracts, foreign contracts, security contracts that clear to margin or guarantee or settle a commodity contract.
- Perfection of a lien within 10 days of the bankruptcy, if within state law, and creditor-transferred property to the debtor within that time.
- Commencement of action by the Department of Housing and Urban Development (HUD) to foreclose a mortgage or deed of trust when five or more living units are involved.
- Reissuance of a tax deficiency by a governmental unit.
- Certain actions by the U.S. Secretary of Commerce under the Ship Mortgage Act or the Merchant Marine Act.

Codebtors and the Automatic Stay   A codebtor (cosigner or guarantor) is never protected from the efforts of a creditor when the debtor files for Chapter 7 or 11 bankruptcy. However, the codebtor has limited protection from the Automatic Stay for Chapters 12 and 13 bankruptcies; there is protection against creditor demands for payment for nonbusiness consumer debts, unless that debt occurred as part of the normal operation of a business by the debtor.

There is partial relief for the codebtor by paying the entire cosigned debt to the creditor. This earns for codebtor the *subrogated* (substituted) right to file a claim for that amount against the debtor.

Overcoming the Automatic Stay   A creditor who wishes to repossess property or to foreclose on it must first file a *Motion to Lift Stay* with the Bankruptcy Court. The creditor must show:

- A specific reason, such as lack of adequate protection for a secured loan.
- Demonstrate that the debtor has no equity in the property, and the property is not necessary for Chapter 11 Reorganization.

Under Chapter 7 bankruptcy, the trustee usually "abandons" property back to the secured creditor if the debtor has no equity in it. During a Chapter 11 bankruptcy, a

Motion to Lift Stay is difficult to win during the first 120 days of the bankruptcy. For Chapters 12 and 13, payments of both past-due and current obligations should begin shortly after the bankruptcy is filed. For Chapter 12, payments for farm land may be limited to the fair rental value of the property.

Court-Controlled Property

The property controlled by the Bankruptcy Court, held available to pay debtor's debts, is called the *Bankruptcy Estate*. It includes:

- All property in which the creditor has a legal or equitable interest, unless exempted (discussed later).
- Interest of both the debtor and debtor's spouse (plus community property), unless legally separate property of the spouse.
- Other property recovered by the bankruptcy trustee based on:
  Excessive bankruptcy attorney fees

  Property turned over to the trustee by a custodian

  Property improperly transferred by the debtor

  Creditor setoffs (credits) against the debtor's account

  Partnership payment rights from individual partners

  Claims arising out of *subordination*
- Property acquired by the debtor within 180 days after the bankruptcy that would have been part of the Bankruptcy Estate if it had been owned by the debtor at that time, received:
  By bequests, devises, or inheritances

  As result of a property settlement included in a divorce decree

  As a beneficiary of a life insurance policy or death benefit
- Proceeds, rents, or profits from property of the bankruptcy estate; Chapters 7 and 11 exclude earnings from services performed by the debtor after the commencement of the bankruptcy; Chapters 12 and 13 include future earnings as part of debt-payment funds to be reimbursed to creditors.

Property Exempt from Control

Not everything held by the debtor becomes part of the Bankruptcy Estate. The Bankruptcy Code allows a number of exemptions to provide a "fresh start" for Chapter 12 and 13 debtors. Or, as an alternative, a number of states have their own exemption lists, which, in most cases, are more generous than those of the federal Bankruptcy Code.

Other exempted property includes that over which the debtor exercises power or authority for the benefit of another, such as a trust established for the debtor's children. Also exempted is any interest in a lease of nonresidential property that expired prior to the commencement of the bankruptcy but where the debtor continues to occupy space, even though the lessor is in a position to regain control of the property.

Personal Property Exemptions

An individual or married couple filing bankruptcy can, as noted earlier, exempt property Congress has deemed essential for a fresh start. The debtor can rely on the Bankruptcy Code exemptions or choose exemptions of property listed by state statutes in those states having such laws.

Exemption does not mean *debt discharge* (termination). While the exempted property is not available in the Bankruptcy Estate to pay prebankruptcy debts (with exceptions, listed later), the property is still subject to liens and must be paid for at the end of the bankruptcy period. For example, exemption for a home from the property to be liquidated under Chapter 7 does not mean that mortgage payments do not need to be paid during the bankruptcy nor does it avoid making up back payments plus interest at the end of the bankruptcy period.

Bankruptcy Code exemptions are:

- Primary residence for the debtor or debtor's dependent, not to exceed $7,500 in value.

- Debtor's interest in one vehicle, not to exceed $1,200; a similar additional exemption for debtor's spouse.

- Debtor's interest in jewelry, not to exceed $500 in value.

- Debtor's interest in any other property, not to exceed $400 in value, in addition to any unused amount of exemption under the personal residence exemption, up to $3,750 in value.

- Debtor's interest in tools of the trade or professional books, not to exceed $750 in value.

- Any unmatured life insurance contract, except for a credit life contract.

- A life insurance policy, not to exceed $4,000 in value.

- Professionally prescribed health aids for the debtor and the debtor's dependents.

- Debtor's right to receive:

    Social Security benefits, unemployment compensation, public assistance benefits

    Veteran's benefits

    Disability, illness, or unemployment benefits

    Alimony, support, or separate maintenance to the extent reasonably necessary to support the debtor

Payment under a stock bonus, pension, profit-sharing annuity, or similar plan based on debtor's illness, disability, death, age, or length of service, with some restrictions

- Debtor's right to receive property as follows:

    As an award under a crime victim's law

    As payment on account of wrongful death

    As payment under a life insurance contract to the extent reasonably necessary for support of the debtor and debtor's dependents

    As payment not to exceed $7,500 on account of personal bodily injury

    As payment in compensation of loss of future earnings of the debtor to the extent reasonably necessary to support the debtor

CREDITORS WHO CAN MAKE CLAIMS

A creditor's *claim* is for the "right of payment, whether or not such right is reduced to judgment, liquidation, unliquidated, fixed, contingent, matured, unmatured, disputed, undisputed, legal, equitable, secured or unsecured." A claim is the right of payment or promise to do work by the debtor and includes disputed claims or a claim contingent on some other event happening. It may include the right to have the debtor perform some previously negotiated or contraction action.

The claim, with some exceptions, must exist at the time of the bankruptcy. The claimant *creditor* can be any entity with a claim against the debtor: a person, a business, a government taxing authority. The types of creditors recognized by bankruptcy law are:

- *Superpriority Creditors.* Those who lend money to the debtor after a Chapter 11 bankruptcy is filed; providers of the money needed to keep the business operating. The loans create liens on any property of the debtor not already subject a lien, or which has a value in excess of the lien. Such creditors are first in line, with secured creditors, for reimbursement.

- *Priority Creditors.* Includes those with wage claims, claims for consumer deposits on goods undelivered by the debtor, and, for a Chapter 11 bankruptcy, claims for the benefits of retirees.

- *Secured Creditors.* Those with security pledges from the debtor of property, accounts receivable, or other items of the debtor's business as security for amounts owed. They are first in line, with priority creditors, for reimbursement.

- *Unsecured Creditors.* Generally those trade creditors or others who sold to the debtor on open accounts without a security interest. These creditors are reimbursed with whatever is left over after secured creditors and priority creditors are paid. Usually, it is not cost-effective for unsecured creditors to file claims unless the claim is large or the cost of filing is minimal.

- *Shareholders and Equity Security Holders.* Those in positions similar to those of secured creditors.

Unpermitted Claims

Some claims are not permitted under the Bankruptcy Code. These include:

- Claims based on legally unenforceable contracts.
- Claims for interest that had not matured on the date that the bankruptcy was filed.
- Property tax claims that exceed the value of the property.
- Claims for services by an *insider* that exceed the reasonable value of such services.
- Claims for alimony, maintenance, or child support not fixed as of the date of bankruptcy filing.
- Claims for excessive penalties for breach of lease.
- Claims based on termination of an employment contract where the amount of the claim exceeds one year's wages.
- All claims filed by a taxing authority that, based on late payments, reduce the amount of credit for payment of employment taxes.

Contesting Claims

In addition to claims that are not allowed under the Bankruptcy Code, other claims may be contested by the debtor, the Bankruptcy Court, or other creditors.

A debtor may object to any claim made by a creditor, and require proof of the claim's validity. If there is no response by the creditor to the debtor's objection, the Bankruptcy Court will deny the claim.

A claim by a creditor is automatically denied if the debtor lists it as disputed or nonliquidated, and the creditor fails to file a timely claim. One creditor may contest the claim made by another creditor.

The Bankruptcy Court allows at least 30 days after an objection to a claim has been filed before it holds a hearing on the objection. When the Bankruptcy Court denies a claim either automatically or after a hearing, the contested claim is eradicated. It no longer exists as a legal obligation for payment.

ORDER OF PAYMENT PRIORITY

If, in a Chapter 11 bankruptcy, the debtor continues to operate the business, and a creditor provides goods and services that are reasonable and necessary for the operation of the business, but the debtor does not pay for them, the creditor is given next to the highest (just under superpriority claims) reimbursement priority.

Following are the claim priorities in the order of priority according to the Bankruptcy Code:

1. Expenses for administering the Bankruptcy Estate incurred after the bankruptcy is filed; includes, for example, attorney and accounting fees.
2. Claims arising during the period between the filing of an involuntary Chapter 7 or 11 bankruptcy against a business, and the Bankruptcy Courts declaration that the business must operate under Bankruptcy Court supervision.
3. Claims for wages, salaries, and commissions earned within 90 days before filing the bankruptcy, up to $2,000 per individual.
4. Claims for money owed employee benefit plans for services rendered within 180 days before filing bankruptcy, up to $2,000 multiplied by the number of employees covered under the plan.
5. Claims by farmers against grain elevators, or fishermen against a cannery or fish-processing plant.
6. Claims for the return of deposits made on consumer goods, not exceeding $900 per individual claimholder.
7. Claims for most taxes.

The priority order for unsecured claims for creditors in Chapter 7 bankruptcies is:

1. Priorities as listed above.
2. Unsecured claims filed within the time period allowed for the bankruptcy.
3. Unsecured claims filed late.
4. Any claim for a penalty, fine, or punitive damages.
5. Payment of interest on any unsecured damages.
6. Payment to the debtor.

Prohibited Payments

The Bankruptcy Court has the authority to void any prohibited payment made by a debtor to a creditor, or other unauthorized transfers of property rightfully included in the Bankruptcy Estate. If such action is taken by the Court, it normally means that the money or the property is returned to the debtor's Bankruptcy Estate so that it can be shared for the benefit of all creditors, not merely one or a few favored creditors.

Preferential Payments   A preferential payment is one made by a debtor to a creditor shortly before the debtor files for bankruptcy. The test is:

- Was the payment made while the debtor was insolvent?
- Was the payment made within 90 days of the bankruptcy filing?

- Was the payment made within one year of bankruptcy if an *insider* was involved?
- Was the payment larger than would have been due the same creditor under a Chapter 7 liquidation?

Nonpreferential Payments Payments that are not considered preferential when made by the debtor include:

- Payments for debts incurred and paid for in the ordinary course of business, according to generally accepted business terms.
- Payments for a contemporaneous exchange of goods for money, or money for goods.
- Transfers of assets that create a security interest in property acquired by the debtor if the security interest secures new value given by the creditor to the debtor.
- Transfers by the debtor that create a security interest in inventory or receivables (subject to certain conditions).
- Payments of less than $600 by an individual debtor whose primary debts are consumer (not business) debts.
- The fixing of certain statutory liens, primarily tax liens.

Insider Payments For a payment by a debtor to be categorized as a payment to an *insider*, the following conditions must exist.

For an individual debtor, the recipient of the payment must be:

- A relative of the debtor or a general partner of the debtor.
- A partnership in which the debtor is a general partner.
- A general partner of the debtor.
- A corporation in which the debtor is a director, officer, or person in control.

For a corporate debtor, the recipient of the payment must be:

- A director of the debtor.
- An officer of the debtor.
- A person in control of the debtor.
- A partnership in which the debtor is a general partner.
- A general partner of the debtor.
- A relative of a general partner, director, officer, or person in charge of the debtor.

For a partnership debtor, the recipient of the payment must be:

- A general partner of the debtor.
- A relative of the general partner or person in control of the debtor.
- A partnership where the debtor is a general partner.
- A person in control of the debtor.

Fraudulent Transfers of Assets   The Bankruptcy Court may order reversal of other money payments or property transfers, namely, those that occur within one year of the bankruptcy filing and were made for fraudulent purposes, such as:

- A transfer made with intent to hinder, delay, or defraud a creditor.
- A transfer made when the debtor is insolvent or becomes insolvent because of it.
- A transfer that gives the debtor less value than would have been reasonable for the exchange.
- A transfer in which the debtor had unreasonably small capital for engaging in the business or the transaction.

HOW CLAIMS ARE FILED

The creditor must file *Proof of Claim* with documents to support the claim. To make the filing, the creditor must know first that a bankruptcy has been filed, either by notice from the debtor or clerk of the Bankruptcy Court, or by a notice or article in a newspaper or trade magazine. When a debtor includes a *matrix* (a mailing list of creditors) with the bankruptcy filing, the clerk of the Bankruptcy Court sends official notice to each of the listed creditors.

The creditor must know the bankruptcy case number and the address of the court for filing the Proof of Claim. In addition, it is helpful to know:

- The name under which the debtor filed bankruptcy.
- The name of the court where the bankruptcy was filed.
- The Chapter type of bankruptcy.
- The filing date.

Filing Bar Date

The *bar date* is the last date on which the Bankruptcy Court will allow a new claim to be filed. If the bar date has been missed, the claim is automatically declared invalid and the debt is discharged or eradicated *if* the creditor knew of the bankruptcy. Bar dates for the four types of bankruptcy are:

- *Chapter 7.* 90 days after the first date set for the creditors' meeting.
- *Chapter 11.* Determined by the Bankruptcy Court. It usually precedes the vote on Reorganization Plan approval.
- *Chapter 12.* 90-day deadline for filing of repayment plan by debtor after filing bankruptcy. The claim should be filed before the debtor drafts the repayment plan.
- *Chapter 13.* 90 days after the first date set for the creditors' meeting.

While bar dates are supposed to be mailed to all known creditors, it is the creditor's responsibility to know the date. Failure to receive notice of a bar date does not bring additional time for the creditor to file a claim.

Tax Claims

Taxation of the debtor is complex, as the Bankruptcy Code is not always crystal clear. In general, taxes owed by an individual survive the bankruptcy (are not discharged) and may affect the debtor long after the case is closed. In contrast, taxes owed by a corporation or partnership in Chapter 7 bankruptcy are discharged or forgiven, as Congress does not want to leave a tax-debit shell for a speculator to purchase.

Tax Debt Forgiveness   The general Internal Revenue Service rule is that the cancellation of a debt is equal to income to the debtor. In bankruptcy, however, debt forgiveness is used to reduce the positive tax position of the debtor and to lessen future tax attributes (i.e., factors used to calculate taxes, as in a depreciation schedule).

Forgiven debt acts to reduce net capital loss for the taxable year in which the debt is discharged and reduces carryover applied to the year of discharge. Forgiven debt reduces the basis for the taxpayer's depreciable assets. The taxpayer may elect to apply all the discharged debt to this category. Forgiven debt also acts to reduce the taxpayer's foreign tax credit.

In summary, forgiven debt tends to lessen certain long-term tax advantages without resulting in immediate income equal to the amount of the forgiven debt.

Seventh Priority Claims and the Internal Revenue Service   As noted earlier, in bankruptcy, your debts are assigned priorities for payment. Most of the tax debts you accumulate before filing for bankruptcy (called prepetition tax debts) are classified as Seventh Priority claims. Prepetition tax debts generally are certain income taxes and other taxes that you are considered to have owed before you filed for bankruptcy protection. Seventh Priority taxes include:

- Income taxes for tax years ending before the date of filing the bankruptcy petition.
- Income taxes assessed within 240 days before the date bankruptcy petition is filed.

- Income taxes assessable as of the date bankruptcy petition is filed.
- Employment taxes on the first $2,000 of income (wages, salaries, commissions) earned by your employees within 90 days or earlier of the "cessation of business" date of filing of the bankruptcy petition.
- Excise taxes for transactions made before the date the bankruptcy petition is filed.

To collect payment for such Seventh Priority tax claims of the Bankruptcy Estate, the IRS must file a timely claim.

Business Taxes

Net Operating Loss (NOL)   If more than 50% of the ownership of the bankrupt corporation or partnership passes to creditors and shareholders during a bankruptcy, the Internal Revenue Code rules that ordinarily apply to limit the amount of NOL to be carried forward are not applicable.

Exchanging Stock for Debt   Generally, the exchange of stock for debt is considered forgiveness of debt and is treated as income to the stock-issuing debtor organization. The exception is when the stock has a minimal value.

"G" Reorganization.   *The Internal Revenue Service recognizes a tax-free "G" reorganization that allows reorganizing corporations to exchange assets for shares and bonds of the corporation that purchases these assets.*

State Corporation Taxes   *State taxes for bankruptcies vary widely by state. Certain state corporation taxes, such as franchise and value-added, may not be granted payment priority.*

According to the Bankruptcy Code in regard to state taxation of bankruptcies, the corporation in bankruptcy must file its own tax returns. For Chapters 7 and 11 bankruptcies, the taxable year ends the day prior to filing the bankruptcy, and a new tax year starts the day after the bankruptcy is filed.

Individual Taxes

Sole Proprietorships   The Internal Revenue Service does not treat debt forgiveness of an individual's debt as income to the individual.

Estate of an Individual   An individual's personal estate is treated as a separate taxable entity for federal income tax purposes. Taxable events in the bankruptcy are covered in a tax report separate from the individual's estate. When the bankruptcy is closed, most tax attributes incurred during the bankruptcy become the property of the individual filing for the bankruptcy.

Personal Services Income   After filing for bankruptcy, personal services income (wages, salary, draw from personal business or partnership) is not subject to the special rules of bankruptcy taxation. Thus, the individual's income from such services is not taxable as part of the Bankruptcy Estate.

State Income Taxes   Income (not including income from personal services) after filing for Chapter 7 or 11 bankruptcies is taxed to the Bankruptcy Estate, not to the individual. In Chapter 13, all income is taxed as income of the individual for state tax liability. For Chapters 7 and 11, the individual's state income tax year stops when the bankruptcy is filed.

Business Taxes and Individuals   Withholding taxes deducted from employee's paychecks may become the individual responsibility of those who control the bankrupt business. For example, officers or directors may be assessed a penalty up to 100% of the unpaid withholding taxes during the year. State sales taxes collected by businesses are usually considered as held in trust for the state by the debtor.

Tax Priorities   A tax claim in bankruptcy ordinarily has priority over a general unsecured claim. Certain state taxes, such as franchise and value-added taxes, may not be granted payment priority.

Taxes Accrued after Bankruptcy   Taxes assessed after the debtor is in bankruptcy are payable when due, even though, as in Chapter 7, the business is no longer operating. Failure to pay taxes while in Chapter 11 may result in a forced conversion from Chapter 11 to Chapter 7. Failure to pay can result in the bankruptcy case being dismissed by the Bankruptcy Court.

Tax Debts and Debt Discharge   As noted elsewhere, most taxes assessed against an individual are not discharged by bankruptcy and remain collectible after the bankruptcy case is closed, along with penalties and interest. Taxes against an on-going corporation or partnership (the Bankruptcy Code treats partnerships like corporations regarding taxes) are discharged through Chapter 11 bankruptcy, but not Chapter 7 bankruptcy.

A tax assessment involving fraud or for which the taxpayer failed to file a tax return is not discharged.

THE CREDITORS' COMMITTEE

Creditors' committees are usually formed for Chapters 7 and 11. However, because of the complexity and expenses involved, most Chapter 11 bankruptcies do not have creditors' committees unless there is a large number of creditors with significant claims. A creditors' committee is even more rare for a Chapter 7 bankruptcy, and there is never a committee for Chapters 12 and 13 bankruptcies.

Membership of the creditors' committee is made up of general unsecured creditors. The objective is to negotiate with the debtor to achieve the best plan and payment schedule to reimburse unsecured creditors. If formed, the creditors' committee is usually the main negotiating party during the preparation of a Chapter 11 Reorganization Plan. A similar committee of *shareholders* may be formed to represent the interests of equityholders of the debtor business.

Normally, either the Bankruptcy Court or the *U.S. Trustee* will appoint 7 or so unsecured creditors, selecting those with the largest claims, to the committee. If there are fewer than 12 unsecured creditors, the committee may consist of only one representative.

The committee members pool resources to hire attorneys and other support services. Activities of the committee can include:

- Consultation with the bankruptcy Trustee or *Debtor-in-Possession* (the Chapter 11 debtor operating the business).
- Investigation of the debtor's actions, liabilities, and report of financial condition.
- Involvement with the debtor and trustee in formulating a Reorganization Plan.

THE CULMINATION OF BANKRUPTCY

The objective of bankruptcy is relief from the burden of debts that exceeds the ability to make payments. In Chapter 7 bankruptcy, this relief is achieved by liquidation of nonexempt assets (sale and conversion to money) with the distribution to reimburse the creditors. In Chapter 11 bankruptcy, the debtor is given time to reorganize under a plan. As much as possible of the debt is paid, with the remainder of the debts being eradicated by discharge. The concept is similar in Chapters 12 and 13.

When Claims Are Paid

Only undisputed claims by creditors are paid, and then only with approval by the Bankruptcy Court. Claim payments are made by the trustee after deducting for trustee fees and bankruptcy administrative expenses for Chapters 7, 12, and 13. There are normally no trustee fees for a Chapter 11 bankruptcy in which the debtor (as the Debtor-in-Possession) does not charge a trustee's fee. Other aspects of payment are:

- *Chapter 7*. Trustee pays claims after the Bankruptcy Estate is liquidated by sale or auction.
- *Chapter 11*. Payments are made in accord with the payment plan. It may take two or more years before the plan is approved.
- *Chapter 12*. Payments are made to the trustee in accord with the payment plan, which is to be filed with the Bankruptcy Court within 90 days of the

bankruptcy filing. The trustee disburses payments to the creditors. Payments extend over three years, unless the Bankruptcy Court "for cause" extends it to five years.

- *Chapter 13.* Payments are made to the trustee in accord with the payment plan, which is to be filed with the Bankruptcy Court within 15 days of the bankruptcy filing. The trustee disburses payments to the creditors. Payments extend over three years, unless the Bankruptcy Court "for cause" extends it to five years.

Discharge of Debts

Discharge of debts is the primary reason for a bankruptcy. Debt that is eliminated by the Bankruptcy Court no longer exists. The creditor cannot take any legal action to collect a discharged debt. Only a moral obligation survives. The creditor cannot file suit, and an offset for the debtor's account is prohibited.

When Debt Discharge Occurs Discharge for Chapter 7 bankruptcy takes effect immediately after the time expires for the creditor to file a complaint to a specific discharge. In most instances, the period allowed to file a complaint expires 90 days after the bankruptcy is filed.

Discharge for Chapter 11 bankruptcy is at the time the Reorganization Plan is confirmed, usually about six months after the bankruptcy is filed. But there is no mandatory time limit for proposing the Reorganization Plan, and the process can drag on for several years.

Discharge for Chapters 12 and 13 is at the completion of payments under the terms of the plan. While this is usually over a three-year period, the court may, for cause, extend payments to a five-year period. In hardship cases, the court may allow discharge even though plan payments are not completed.

In general, if a creditor wishes to have a debt survive the bankruptcy process, a notice must be filed with the Bankruptcy Court within the permitted time period. No hearing is required, however, for taxes against the debtor or for child support, and such.

Debts That Are Not Discharged In general, a lien on a bankrupt debtor's property by a secured creditor is *tolled* (held in abeyance) during the bankruptcy. To keep the property, the debtor must arrange to pay for it.

Prior to discharge, a debtor may *reaffirm* the debt on property on which there is a lien and which the debtor wants to keep. In such a case, the lien survives the discharge. The value for reaffirmation is usually that which exists at the time of the bankruptcy, not the original contract price.

Debts that are not discharged by bankruptcy for individuals and that face collection action after the bankruptcy case terminates include those attributed to:

- Taxes or custom duties, generally those accruing within three years or less of the bankruptcy.

- Fraud: receipt of money, property, or services by false pretenses, false representations, *actual fraud*.
- *Materially* false financial statements involving money, property, services, or credit.
- Alimony and child support, debt to a spouse or former spouse or child.
- Debts the debtor failed to list on the bankruptcy schedule (these cannot be discharged unless the debtor can prove that the creditors involved knew of the bankruptcy in time to file a claim).

Except for Chapter 13 bankruptcy, as discussed in the next chapter, there is no discharge for debts attributed to:

- Larceny, embezzlement, or *defalcation* by a *fiduciary*.
- Willful and malicious injury to another by the debtor.
- Fines, penalties, or forfeitures due the government or other tax penalty.
- Educational loans guaranteed by a governmental unit.
- A judgment involving debtor's operation of a motor vehicle while intoxicated.

CHAPTER 4

THE BANKRUPTCY PROCESS

GETTING STARTED

The debtor may choose the most convenient location, as long as for 180 days before filing the debtor meets at least one of the following:

- The debtor's domicile or residency is in the location served by the Bankruptcy Court.
- The debtor's primary place of business is in the location served by the Bankruptcy Court.
- The debtor's principal assets are in the location served by the Bankruptcy Court. With multiple asset or business locations, the debtor will have more than one choice.

FILING FOR BANKRUPTCY

A bankruptcy is started by filing a *Petition for Relief* with the Bankruptcy Court, followed within 15 days by filing the *Bankruptcy Schedule*, a list of the debtor's assets and debts. The schedule should be accompanied by copies of recent tax returns, payments to creditors made within 90 days of the bankruptcy filing, and a list of creditors with their addresses and the amounts owed to them. If this list is alphabetical, it is called the *matrix*. If there is a problem preparing the schedule in time, the debtor can petition the Bankruptcy Court for an extension for cause.

FILING FEES

The following fees were in effect in 1992:

- Chapter 7 or 12 or 13 $120.00
- Chapter 11 $500.00
- Notice of Appeal $105.00

CHAPTER 7 LIQUIDATION BANKRUPTCY

Sequence of a Chapter 7 Bankruptcy

1. The Petition for Relief is filed by the debtor.
2. The Automatic Stay takes effect.
3. The Schedule (assets and debts) is filed by debtor.
4. The Clerk of the Bankruptcy Court notifies creditors listed by the debtor of the bankruptcy.
5. The interim trustee is appointed by the Bankruptcy Court or the U.S. Trustee.
6. The First Meeting of the creditors is held, and creditors elect a permanent trustee.
7. Creditors may form a creditors' committee (not done for every bankruptcy).
8. Each creditor files its claim(s).
9. Debtor and trustee determine which property will be included in the Bankruptcy Estate, which is exempt, and which debts will be reaffirmed for redemption by the debtor.
10. The trustee seeks out and gathers additional assets that belong in the Bankruptcy Estate.
11. The trustee liquidates assets included in the Bankruptcy Estate, by sale or public auction.
12. The trustee distributes the proceeds of the liquidation to qualified creditors according to their priorities.
13. The Bankruptcy Court discharges the debtor from the remaining unpaid debts.
14. The trustee files final accountings with the Bankruptcy Court.
15. The Bankruptcy Court closes the case.

Chapter 7 Bankruptcy in General

The objective of the Chapter 7 bankruptcy process is to terminate debts by liquidating all nonexempt assets through sale or auction. A trustee is appointed with control over (ownership of) all qualifying assets. Proceeds of the liquidation sale are used to pay the cost of administration and trustee's fees, and reimburse approved creditors, at least partially.

Chapter 7 Liquidation is usually filed by businesses or individuals with financial conditions beyond help through Reorganization (Chapter 11) or personal debt-payment plans (Chapters 12 or 13). Chapter 7 bankruptcy may be filed voluntarily by (or involuntarily for, when forced by a creditor) a debtor, including:

- Individuals and married couples.
- Partnerships.
- Corporations.
- Joint-stock companies.
- Virtually any other business, with restrictions for railroads, insurance companies, banks, savings banks, credit unions.

Starting the Process

The process starts when the debtor files the *Petition for Relief* with the Bankruptcy Court. Administration of the bankruptcy by the Bankruptcy Court begins when (if) the judge holds that there is sufficient reason for the bankruptcy and enters the *Order for Relief*. For a corporation or other business, all activity ceases, although the court can allow the business to continue operations under the control of the trustee if it will facilitate a more orderly liquidation of the assets.

The Bankruptcy Trustee

When the Chapter 7 petition is filed, the bankruptcy judge or the *U.S. Trustee* will appoint an Interim Trustee for the case to oversee the bankruptcy process. This trustee has legal control over all the property in the Bankruptcy Estate. A primary task of the trustee is to locate and gain possession of additional assets that belong in the Bankruptcy Estate, such as unpermitted insider payments and preferential payments to selected creditors.

At the *First Meeting of the Creditors*, the creditors elect a permanent trustee. Only those creditors with undisputed claims can vote at this time. The trustee then queries the debtor about the accuracy of the schedules (assets and debts) filed with the Bankruptcy Court, and determines if there are any hidden problems. In general, the trustee will:

- Collect the Bankruptcy Estate property, and convert it to cash.
- Account for all property received.
- Ensure that the debtor lists property exempt from the bankruptcy.
- Declare which debts are to be reaffirmed.
- Investigate the financial affairs of the debtor.

- Examine proofs of claim by the creditors and object to any improper claims.
- Oppose (if desirable) proofs of claims.
- Provide information about the bankruptcy to claimholders and equityholders, unless otherwise ordered by the Court.
- File tax returns if the business continues to operate.
- File a final report and accounting of the administration of the bankruptcy.

The trustee may hire attorneys, accountants, appraisers, or other professionals to fulfill the duties of trusteeship.

Property and Individual Bankruptcies

As for business bankruptcies, the property and other assets of the individual or married-couple debtor are surveyed to determine which will be part of the Bankruptcy Estate, which will be exempt from liquidation, and which will be redeemed by the debtor via debt reaffirmation and payment. The trustee may abandon assets back to the lien-holding creditor (not include them for liquidation as part of the Bankruptcy Estate) when the property value is equal to the lien value.

As noted earlier, individuals and married couples filing Chapter 7 bankruptcy may exempt certain properties from the liquidation process when such properties qualify as necessary for a "fresh start" under the Federal Bankruptcy Code or individual state statutes, whichever is most favorable to the debtor. This type of fresh-start exemption is not allowed when businesses file for Chapter 7 bankruptcy.

Consumer items (in contrast to business assets) may be redeemed (removed from the liquidation process) by the individual or married-couple debtor if the debtor reaffirms the debt on property on which there is a lien claim by the creditor, and pays or agrees to pay the amount of the lien. Similarly, the debtor may redeem property abandoned by the trustee and not included in the Bankruptcy Estate. Such redemptions must be approved by the Bankruptcy Court.

All property not abandoned back to the lienholders and which the individual or married-couple debtor does not claim as exempt is liquidated. The proceeds of the liquidation are distributed to the creditors according to their priority classification.

Distribution of Liquidation Funds

After the trustee liquidates the Bankruptcy Estate by sale or public auction or other means, the resulting funds are disbursed in the following priority order:

1. Secured claims in accordance with their securities.
2. Administrative expenses after the bankruptcy is filed.
3. Involuntary gap claims; claims occurring during the period between an involuntary bankruptcy filing forced on the debtor by a creditor and the issuance of an Order for Relief by the Bankruptcy Court.

4. Claims for wages, salaries, and commissions that were earned within 90 days before the bankruptcy filing, up to a maximum of $2,000 per individual claimant.

5. Claims for employee benefit plans rendered within 180 days before the bankruptcy filing, up to a maximum of $2,000 per number of employees in the plan.

6. Claims by farmers against grain elevators, and claims by fishermen against canners or fish-producing plants.

7. Claims for return of deposits for consumer goods, not to exceed $900 per claimant.

8. Claims for most taxes.

9. Unsecured claims filed within the allotted time period.

10. Unsecured claims that were filed late.

11. Claims for penalties, fines, or punitive damages.

12. Interest payments on any unsecured claim.

13. Payment to the debtor.

Discharge of Debts

Discharge (termination) of debt liability for unpaid debts under Chapter 7 bankruptcy is granted to individual and married-couple debtors only. There is no need for debt discharge for businesses, since they no longer operate following Chapter 7 Liquidation. Perhaps equally important, Congress wanted to avoid trades in shell businesses with huge tax losses but no current debt or assets.

A creditor can contest the discharge of any debt by filing a complaint with the Bankruptcy Court within 60 days of the First Meeting of the Creditors. Or the Bankruptcy Court on its own may deny the discharge of a debt for an individual or married-couple debtor if during or within one year prior to the bankruptcy or within one year following the granting of the discharge:

1. The debtor defrauded creditors or the trustee by:

   concealing property,

   wrongfully removing property,

   wrongfully transferring property, or

   wrongfully destroying property.

2. The debtor, unless justified under the circumstances:

   destroyed records,

   mutilated records,

   falsified records, or

   failed to keep records or papers from which the creditor or trustee could ascertain business transactions.

3. The debtor during the bankruptcy:

    made a false oath,

    presented a false claim,

    withheld information or records from the trustee or Bankruptcy Court,

    performed a fraudulent act in return for money or the promise of money, or

    failed to explain the loss of an asset.

4. The debtor refused during the bankruptcy to:

    obey an order from the Bankruptcy Court, or

    answer a *material question* if the Bankruptcy Court has granted immunity against self-incrimination.

5. The debtor within six years of filing the bankruptcy:

    received a Chapter 11 bankruptcy discharge, or

    received a Chapter 12 or 13 bankruptcy discharge, unless 70% of all claims were paid and the payment plan was proposed in good faith.

The Bankruptcy Court may authorize a denial of discharge on a debt-by-debt basis.

Closing the Case

The Automatic Stay protection for the Chapter 7 debtors ends when the debtor's debts are discharged. The Automatic Stay protection for the property and assets in the Bankruptcy Estate ends when the trustee completes the liquidation process. In total, the Automatic Stay is terminated when the case is closed or dismissed by the Bankruptcy Court.

After completion of the liquidation, the trustee files a final report to the Bankruptcy Court of proposed distribution of the money gained through the liquidation. The report accounts for all of the property and other assets in the Bankruptcy Estate, and files for payment of trustee fees. The case is normally closed by the clerk of the Bankruptcy Court after receiving the court's order approving the trustee's final report.

CHAPTER 11 REORGANIZATION BANKRUPTCY

Sequence of a Chapter 11 Bankruptcy

1. The Petition for Relief is filed with the Bankruptcy Court.

2. The Automatic Stay takes effect.

3. The debtor (called the *Debtor-in-Possession* or *DIP*) continues to run the business.

4. The DIP seeks permission from the Bankruptcy Court to use cash collateral to support operation of the business.

5. The DIP files its Schedule (assets and debts) and matrix list of specific creditors and amounts owed.

6. The Clerk of the Bankruptcy Court notifies listed creditors of the bankruptcy.

7. The First Meeting of the Creditors is held.

8. Each creditor files its claim(s).

9. Creditors' committees may be formed.

10. Shareholder/equityholder committees may be formed.

11. Creditor claims are allowed or disallowed.

12. The Bankruptcy Court appoints a trustee or, if the debtor has engaged in mismanagement or fraud, an examiner.

13. The Disclosure Statement is filed.

14. The DIP (or the creditors) files the Reorganization Plan.

15. Creditors decide to support or object to the debtor's Disclosure Statement and Reorganization Plan.

16. The Bankruptcy Court approves or disapproves the Disclosure Statement.

17. Creditors and shareholders vote on the Reorganization Plan.

18. The Bankruptcy Court confirms or rejects the Reorganization Plan.

19. If the Bankruptcy Court confirms the Reorganization Plan, the court retains control over the case only to implement the plan.

20. When reorganization under the plan is complete, the Bankruptcy Court closes the case.

21. If the reorganization under the plan fails, the case is converted from Chapter 11 Reorganization to Chapter 7 Liquidation.

Chapter 11 Bankruptcy in General

The Chapter 11 Reorganization is the dominant type of bankruptcy for business in general. The purpose is to gain temporary relief from paying past debts, giving the debtor time to reorganize, pay creditors (at least partially), and emerge from the bankruptcy as a financially viable entity.

While either a business of virtually any size or type or an individual can file for Chapter 11 Reorganization, the process can be complex and costly, particularly if there is a large number of creditors, each with multiple claims against the debtor. If the enterprise seeking Chapter 11 protection comprises several business organizations or subsidiaries, each must make its own bankruptcy filing. Chapter 11 is not available to stock or commodity brokers or municipalities.

Mostly, large businesses file under Chapter 11. If the reorganization fails, or if the attempt to create a Reorganization Plan fails, the Chapter 11 Reorganization may be converted to a Chapter 7 Liquidation.

The debtor attempts to draft a Reorganization Plan that will be accepted by both the majority of the creditors and the Bankruptcy Court. If the debtor's efforts fail, the creditors may attempt to draft a plan. If both fail, the next step is to convert the Chapter 11 petition to a Chapter 7 petition.

After the Reorganization Plan has been approved and adopted, the debtor's debt repayments are limited to those specifically listed by the plan. Meanwhile, the business continues to operate during the bankruptcy, usually under the control of the debtor. Many Chapter 11 Reorganizations last for several years, or more.

Creditors' Meeting

The first meeting of the creditors, also known as a *341 Meeting* after Section 341 of the Bankruptcy Code, is usually held within the first few weeks of the bankruptcy filing. The purpose of the meeting is to provide an opportunity for the creditors and the debtor to negotiate, preliminary to drafting a Reorganization Plan.

The creditors will ask probing questions, seeking to determine in detail the locations dispositions of assets, and to investigate disputed debts. The judge of the Bankruptcy Court is not allowed to attend this meeting.

The Debtor-in-Possession

Debtor-in-Possession (or DIP) describes the situation where, in a Chapter 11 bankruptcy, the debtor who has filed for bankruptcy remains in possession of and control of the property and assets involved. This is directly opposite to Chapter 7 bankruptcy in which a trustee "owns" the property assets of the Bankruptcy Estate for the purpose of liquidation.

The DIP therefore acts as its own trustee with all the power and authority of a trustee. The DIP usually continues to operate the business, largely without interference from the Bankruptcy Court, for the benefit of both itself and of the creditors. The DIP may continue any activity in the ordinary course of business without seeking special approval from the Bankruptcy Court.

For exceptional matters, such as selling or purchasing a major asset, court approval is needed. Other situations that require court approval include obtaining credit to operate the business, converting cash collateral into operating funds, assuming or rejecting an unexpired lease, or employing professional services, such as attorneys, accountants, or appraisers.

Basic differences between the DIP acting in a trustee role and a trustee in Liquidation bankruptcy include:

- The DIP does not receive a trustee fee.
- The DIP normally does not make monthly payments to creditors.

- The DIP is not appointed by the Bankruptcy Court.
- The DIP is not an officer of the court.

Although highly unusual, the Bankruptcy Court may appoint a trustee to take over the duties and responsibilities of the DIP when actions prior to or during the bankruptcy are fraudulent, dishonest, or incompetent, or where there is gross mismanagement by current management, or other causes. A lesser recourse is the appointment of an examiner to investigate the DIP's business.

Financing Operations

One of the first needs for the business while under Chapter 11 Reorganization is operating cash for purchases, salaries, supplies, and other business expenses. This is usually accomplished by one or both of two approaches, each of which requires court approval.

Cash collateral can be pledged to a lender, such as a bank, as security for a line of credit. Cash collateral is defined as:

- Accounts receivable.
- Cash on hand.
- *Negotiable instruments.*
- Documents to title.
- Securities.
- Deposit accounts.
- Proceeds from property.
- Rents.
- Offspring (includes products from inventory and crops).

The Bankruptcy Code encourages lenders to accept cash collateral as security for a credit line by granting a *superpriority* lien position for lenders to Chapter 11 debtors.

The Reorganization Plan

For 20 days, the DIP has the exclusive right to file a Reorganization Plan. It must be approved within 180 days. After that, a claim-holding creditor or other party may file a plan.

The plan can be simple or complex. Basically, it must contain:

- Designation of each class of claims.
- Whether or not a claim class or claim is *impaired*.
- Treatment of an impaired claim or claim class.

- Provision for uniform treatment of claims in the same class.
- Provisions to implement the plan.

The Disclosure Statement   A Disclosure Statement must accompany the Reorganization Plan. It must contain information needed to guide the creditors as they consider their vote; namely the financial condition of the debtor, why the business failed, reasons for the proposed Reorganization Plan, and a summary of the plan.

Accepting the Reorganization Plan   Following submittal of the Disclosure Statement, the creditors vote on the reorganization plan. To be accepted, it must be approved by a majority of creditors and others with financial interests. *Unimpaired creditors* must accept the reorganization plan; they cannot vote against it.

Once the plan has been approved, the Bankruptcy Court can confirm it with a Confirmation Hearing. The court must approve the Disclosure Statement and must be assured that all creditors and shareholders have been notified of the disclosure statement, reorganization plan, and confirmation hearing.

The Court may *cram down* the plan on a creditor class that does not accept the plan, just as long as the Court considers the Plan to be fair and equitable to that class. Cram-down is assisted when the debtor's reorganization plan groups into a single class those creditors most likely to register complaints.

Operating under Chapter 11

Active involvement by the Bankruptcy Court ends with confirmation of the reorganization plan. Its only role then is to enforce compliance with the plan. After confirmation and adoption of the plan, there is no protection against new debts by the debtor, and the DIP may be sued in state court. Only the underlying debts listed in the plan remain. The rest of the debts are discharged.

As for a Chapter 7 bankruptcy, a creditor who wishes to foreclose on or otherwise retrieve property or an asset listed as part of the Bankruptcy Estate is held in abeyance by the Automatic Stay. To foreclose, the creditor must file a *Motion to Lift Stay* with the Bankruptcy Court.

During the Chapter 11 bankruptcy, the DIP must attempt good-faith negotiation to resolve labor-union contract disputes. If negotiation fails, the DIP must have court approval to reject the contract.

As an exception to other types of prebankruptcy debts, the DIP is allowed to continue a commitment to pay an insurance premium for retiree benefits during bankruptcy, even before the Reorganization Plan is approved.

For sale of property, the Bankruptcy Court can order that the DIP sell "free and clear of liens," even for property on which a creditor holds a lien. This court order facilitates the sale by removing the lien from the property while allowing the creditor to attach a lien to the sale proceeds.

The DIP is not prohibited from trading securities during a Chapter 11 bankruptcy and may trade its stocks and bonds.

The DIP is not, however, protected from a governmental order to stop polluting or to clean up an environmental problem. The order still holds when the debtor emerges from bankruptcy.

CHAPTER 12 FAMILY-FARMER BANKRUPTCY

Sequence of a Chapter 12 Bankruptcy

1. Debtor files Petition for Relief.
2. Automatic Stay takes effect.
3. A trustee is appointed by the Bankruptcy Court.
4. Debtor files Schedule of assets and debts, and list of creditors.
5. The clerk of the Bankruptcy Court notifies creditors of the bankruptcy.
6. The debtor files a plan of payments.
7. First meeting of creditors is held.
8. Each creditor files its claim(s).
9. Trustee and creditors decide to accept or reject the plan of payments.
10. The Bankruptcy Court confirms or denies the plan.
11. The trustee collects the debtor's payments under the plan.
12. The trustee disburses payments to the creditors.
13. At end of plan period, debtor's debts are discharged.
14. The Automatic Stay ends.
15. The trustee submits a final report to the court.
16. The case is closed.

Chapter 12 Bankruptcy in General

Family-Farmer bankruptcy law is relatively new, established by Congress in 1986. It combines some elements of a Chapter 11 bankruptcy with the Chapter 13 Wage-Earner bankruptcy. Chapter 12 bankruptcy is limited to a family-owned agricultural business. As in Chapter 11 Reorganization, the debtor farmer continues to operate the farm or business during bankruptcy.

After the debtor files for Chapter 12 protection, the Bankruptcy Court appoints a trustee to work with the debtor to draft a payment plan, then to collect payments from the debtor for reimbursement of the creditors. The plan is for a three-year period, although the court can extend it to five years for cause. At the end of the period, all remaining debts (except those that were exempted from the plan) are discharged. During this period, the debtor keeps and operates the property, using proceeds to pay creditors. Meanwhile, cosigners/guarantors for the debtor's consumer (not business) debt are protected from liability.

To be eligible for Chapter 12 Family-Farmer relief:

- An individual or married couple may file if 50% or more of their income is based on farming or agricultural operations.
- Total debts may not exceed $1.5 million.
- 80% of nonhome debts must arise from the farming or agricultural operation.
- Corporate ownership of at least 50% held by one family that operates the farm or agricultural operation may file if 50% or more of family income is based on farming or agricultural operations.

A Chapter 12 bankruptcy cannot be involuntary; it cannot be forced by a creditor. The bankruptcy and Automatic Stay protection begin on the date the bankruptcy petition is filed.

The Chapter 12 Payment Plan

The payment plan is akin to a budget, listing essential personal expenses, essential farming expenses, current income, outstanding debts, and disposable income available to pay creditors. With these figures at hand, the debtor proposes a payment schedule, stating how much will be paid to each creditor on a monthly basis. Payments are to be based on creditor priority and classification.

A well-planned bankruptcy is filed at the same time that the debtor files the Petition for Relief with the Bankruptcy Court. At most, it must be filed within 90 days of the filing for bankruptcy, unless the court permits a time extension for cause.

Plan Contents   To be acceptable, the minimum allowable that the payment plan must provide is:

- Debtor to pay trustee all or most of future disposable income.
- All priority claims to be paid in full.
- Treatment to be similar for each creditor within each separate class of general, unsecured creditors.

Other provisions that may be included in the payment plan include:

- Special payment schedule for certain unsecured claims for consumer goods for which a person other than the debtor cosigned or guaranteed.
- Curing or waiving of any default.
- Modification of the rights of a secured creditor.
- Full or partial payment of taxes or consumer debts that accrue after filing for bankruptcy, but prior to confirmation of the payment plan.
- Assumption, rejection, or assignment of unexpired leases assumed by the debtor.

- Cure of any default on a claim for which the final payment is due after the final payment proposed under the payment plan.
- Liquidation of the Bankruptcy Estate and disbursement of the proceeds to creditors.
- Payment of a secured claim over a time period longer than the length of the payment plan.

A secured creditor must accept the payment plan if it is to be binding on that creditor, *unless* the following provisions are included in the plan:

- The creditor is allowed to retain its lien.
- The value to be disbursed to the creditor will be at least equal to the amount of the creditor's allowed claim.
- The property is returned to the creditor if the creditor is not allowed the benefits of the first two provisions.

The payment plan may be modified prior to confirmation by the Bankruptcy Court, or after confirmation but before completion of payments under the plan. Modification may be requested by the debtor, the trustee, or the holder of an unsecured claim. The modified plan must meet the same standards required for the original plan.

Plan Confirmation   Within 45 days of date the payment plan is filed, the Bankruptcy Court confirms or rejects the plan after a hearing with the trustee and those creditors who have objected to the plan. A secured creditor who refuses to accept the plan may continue to rely on its original security agreement. Any unsecured creditor not included in the plan is no longer owed by the debtor.

The court looks for a good-faith proposal that will distribute to the unsecured creditors at least as much as would be distributed by a Chapter 7 Liquidation. Once the payment plan has been confirmed, it becomes binding on the debtor, the trustee, and all the unsecured creditors.

The Chapter 12 Bankruptcy Estate

The definition of contents for a Chapter 12 Bankruptcy Estate is the same as the expanded definition of property for a Chapter 13 bankruptcy, discussed in detail in the next section. In general, the Bankruptcy Estate includes:

- All income after filing for bankruptcy from personal services performed by the debtor.
- Property acquired after filing for bankruptcy, provided it would not have been exempt had the debtor owned it at the time the bankruptcy was filed.

Not included in the Bankruptcy Estate are the "fresh start" exemptions allowed by the Bankruptcy Code, discussed earlier, or those provided by state statutes where the debtor has residency.

The Chapter 12 Trustee

The trustee's main function is to collect payments from the debtor and disburse them to the creditors according to the payment plan, after deducting trustee fees.

The trustee maintains detailed records of payments and disbursements but does not take control or possession of the debtor's farm or other assets. Meanwhile, the debtor continues to operate the business.

The Bankruptcy Court may request that the trustee investigate the business to recommend the desirability (or lack of it) as a continuing operation, and to develop information relevant to formulating a plan. The trustee advises the court as to the value of property subject to liens, if the proposed sale of property is for a reasonable price, and whether or not the court should confirm or modify a payment plan.

If the debtor ceases operation of the farm, the trustee may continue to operate it. The trustee will then have the responsibility of filing all necessary tax returns.

Other duties and responsibilities of the trustee include:

- Seeing that debtor lists property exempt from the bankruptcy.
- Seeing that debtor declares which debts will be reaffirmed.
- Examining proofs of creditor claims; objecting if they are improper.
- If advisable, opposing the discharge of the debtor.
- Furnishing information about the debtor to claimholders and shareholders, unless ordered otherwise by the court.

Discharge of Debts

The discharge of debts for a Chapter 12 bankruptcy more nearly compares with that for a Chapter 7 or 11 than it does Chapter 13. All debts are discharged except:

- Debts included in the payment plan for which the last payment is due after the date on which the plan is completed.
- Taxes assessed against an individual.
- Debts induced by fraud.
- Debts induced by use of false financial statements.
- Debts based on embezzlement or larceny.
- Alimony and child support.
- Government-guaranteed educational loans.

The Bankruptcy Court may make a hardship discharge, even if the debtor has failed to complete payments according to the plan. The debtor must show that the failure was for reasons for which "the Debtor should not justly be held accountable." Even so, the payments must have exceeded the amount that would have been paid under a Chapter 7 Liquidation.

If, within 180 days of granting discharge, the court learns that it was obtained by fraud, the court may revoke the discharge.

CHAPTER 13 WAGE-EARNER BANKRUPTCY

Sequence of a Chapter 13 Bankruptcy

1. Debtor files Petition for Relief.
2. Automatic Stay takes effect.
3. A trustee is appointed by the Bankruptcy Court.
4. Debtor files schedule of assets and debts, and list of creditors.
5. The Clerk of the Bankruptcy Court notifies creditors of the bankruptcy.
6. The debtor files a plan of payments.
7. The first meeting of creditors is held.
8. Each creditor files its claim(s).
9. Trustee and creditors decide to accept or reject the plan.
10. The Bankruptcy Court confirms or denies the plan.
11. The trustee collects the debtor's payments under the plan.
12. The trustee disburses payments to the creditors.
13. At the end of the plan period, debtor's debts are discharged.
14. The Automatic Stay ends.
15. The trustee submits a final report to the court.
16. The case is closed.

Chapter 13 Bankruptcy in General

There were more than one million Chapter 13 bankruptcy filings during 1991. The primary objective of Wage-Earner bankruptcy is to relieve persons or small personal businesses of overwhelming debt burdens, and give a chance for a fresh start. As for the Family-Farmer bankruptcy, a plan is prepared for at least partial reimbursement of creditors over a three-year period, at the end of which those debts not fully paid are discharged. Chapter 13 also protects cosigners/guarantors against claims for consumer (not business) debts of the bankrupt party.

Filing for Chapter 13 bankruptcy can forestall foreclosures or repossessions by un-paid creditors. The wage-earner is not forced to sell off essential assets, and, in the case of a business, the debtor can continue to operate that business. Contrary to a Chapter 7 Liquidation, the trustee does not control the debtor's assets. The major purpose and duty of the trustee is to collect payments from the debtor and disburse them to the listed creditors.

Chapter 13 bankruptcy applies to individuals or married couples, as well as sole proprietorships if the business is owned by the individual filing for bankruptcy. It allows payments over a period of time without forced liquidation of assets essential for a fresh start. The money paid to the creditors must, however, be at least equal to what the creditors would have received under a Chapter 7 Liquidation bankruptcy.

To be eligible for Chapter 13 Wage-Earner relief:

- The applicant cannot be a corporation.
- Secured debt may not exceed $350,000.
- Unsecured debt may not exceed $100,000.
- The party filing must have income (salary, wages, or regular draw from personal business) that is sufficiently stable to allow regular payments under a plan.

The Chapter 13 Payment Plan

A well-prepared plan will be ready at the time the Petition for Relief is filed with the Bankruptcy Court but must be filed within 15 days of filing, unless the court allows more time. You will note the similarity of the Chapter 13 payment plan approach to that of a Chapter 12 payment plan. In brief:

- The payment plan is akin to a budget, listing expenses, income, debts, and disposable income available to pay creditors.
- The debtor proposes the payment plan schedule, specifying how much will be paid monthly to each creditor.
- Payments are calculated on the basis of creditor priority and claim classification.
- All priority claims are to be paid in full.
- Each secured creditor must accept the plan voluntarily for it to be binding; otherwise the creditor can rely on the original security agreement.
- To make the plan binding on a secured creditor:

    It must allow the secured creditor to retain its lien;

    The value distributed to the secured creditor must be at least equal to the value of the property secured by lien; or

    Lacking the preceding two provisions, the plan must provide for the debtor to return the property to the creditor.

- Payments are to be made over a three-year period which, by permission of the court, can be extended to five years.
- The total amount paid to unsecured creditors must be at least equal to what they would have received under a Chapter 7 Liquidation.

Other provisions that may be included in the payment plan include:

- Special payment schedule for certain unsecured claims for consumer goods for which a person other than the debtor cosigned or guaranteed.
- Curing or waiving of any default.
- Modification of the rights of a secured creditor.
- Full or partial payment of taxes or consumer debts that accrue after filing for bankruptcy but prior to confirmation of the payment plan.
- Assumption, rejection, or assignment of unexpired leases assumed by the debtor.
- Cure of any default on a claim for which the final payment is due after the final payment proposed under the payment plan.
- Liquidation of the Bankruptcy Estate and disbursement of the proceeds to creditors.
- Payment of a secured claim over a time period longer than the length of the payment plan.

The payment plan may be modified prior to confirmation by the Bankruptcy Court, or after confirmation but before completion of payments under the plan. Modification may be requested by the debtor, the trustee, or the holder of an unsecured claim. The modified plan must meet the same standards required in the original plan.

Plan Confirmation Within 45 days of date the payment plan is filed, the Bankruptcy Court confirms or rejects the plan after a hearing with the trustee and those creditors who have objected to the plan. A secured creditor who refuses to accept the plan may continue to rely on its original security agreement. Any unsecured creditor not included in the plan is no longer owed by the debtor.

The court looks for a good-faith proposal that will distribute to the unsecured creditors at least as much as would be distributed under a Chapter 7 Liquidation. Once the payment plan is confirmed, it becomes binding on the debtor, the trustee, and all the unsecured creditors.

The Chapter 13 Bankruptcy Estate

The definition of contents for a Chapter 13 Bankruptcy Estate is the same as the definition of property for a Chapter 12 bankruptcy, discussed in detail in the previous section. In general, the Bankruptcy Estate includes:

- All income after filing for bankruptcy from personal services performed by the debtor.
- Property acquired after filing for bankruptcy, provided it would not have been exempt had the debtor owned it at the time the bankruptcy was filed.

Not included in the Bankruptcy Estate are the "fresh start" exemptions allowed by the Bankruptcy Code, discussed earlier, or those provided by state statutes where the debtor has residency.

The Chapter 13 Trustee

The trustee's main function is to collect payments from the debtor, and disburse them to the creditors according to the payment plan, after deducting trustee fees.

The trustee maintains detailed records of payments and disbursements but does not take control or possession of the debtor's personal or business assets. Meanwhile, the debtor continues to operate the business.

The Bankruptcy Court may request that the trustee investigate the business to recommend the desirability (or lack of it) as a continuing operation and to develop information relevant to formulating a plan. The trustee advises the court as to the value of property subject to liens, if a proposed sale of property is for a reasonable price, and whether or not the court should confirm or modify a payment plan.

Other duties and responsibilities of the Trustee include:

- Seeing that debtor lists property exempt from the bankruptcy.
- Seeing that debtor declares which debts will be reaffirmed.
- Examining proofs of creditor claims; objecting if they are improper.
- If advisable, opposing the discharge of the debtor.
- Furnishing information about the debtor to claimholders and shareholders, unless ordered otherwise by the court.

Discharge of Debts

The discharge of debts for a Chapter 13 differs from that of a Chapter 12 bankruptcy. As with Chapter 12, there is no discharge for debts included in the payment plan for which the last payment is due after the date on which the plan is completed, nor is there discharge of payments due to a spouse, former spouse, or child of the debtor for alimony, maintenance, or support.

The major difference between Chapter 12 and 13 is the broad scope of debts discharged under Chapter 13, but not under Chapter 12. These include:

- Taxes assessed against an individual.
- Debts induced by fraud.
- Debts induced by use of false financial statements.
- Debts based on embezzlement or larceny.
- Alimony and child support.
- Government-guaranteed educational loans.

The Bankruptcy Court may make a hardship discharge, even if the debtor has failed to complete payments according to the plan. The debtor must show that the failure was for reasons for which "the Debtor should not justly be held accountable." Even so, the payments must have exceeded the amount that would have been paid under a Chapter 7 Liquidation, and under a hardship discharge, the Chapter 13 debtor is not discharged from taxes or debts induced by fraud or embezzlement.

If, within 180 days of granting discharge, the court learns that it was obtained by fraud, the court may revoke the discharge.

APPENDIXES

APPENDIX I

IRS PUBLICATION

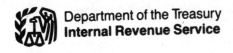

Department of the Treasury
Internal Revenue Service

Publication 908
(Rev. Dec. 88)

Bankruptcy and Other Debt Cancellation

Introduction

This publication covers the federal income tax rules relating to bankruptcy and other cancellations of debt. This revision includes the changes made necessary by the passage of the Technical and Miscellaneous Revenue Act of 1988. For example, that act modified and clarified the rules for excluding from gross income discharges or cancellations of *qualified farm debt*.

The discussions in this publication are limited to the tax aspects of individual and small business debt cancellations. The publication is not intended to cover bankruptcy law in general, or to provide detailed discussions of the tax rules for the more complex corporate bankruptcy reorganizations or other highly technical transactions. In these areas, you should seek competent professional advice.

Cancellation or Forgiveness of Your Debt

General rule. If a debt you owe is cancelled or forgiven, other than as a gift or bequest to you, you generally must include the cancelled amount in your gross income for tax purposes. A debt includes any indebtedness for which you are liable or which attaches to property you hold.

Example. You obtained a mortgage loan on your personal residence several years ago at a relatively low rate of interest. This year, in return for your paying off the loan early, the lending institution cancels a part of the remaining principal. You must include the amount cancelled in your gross income.

Exceptions to General Rule

Purchase-money debt reduction. If you owe a debt to the seller for the purchase of property, and the seller reduces the amount you owe, generally you do not have income from the reduction even though you are not bankrupt or insolvent. The reduction of the debt is treated as a purchase price adjustment, and reduces your basis in the property.

Cancellation of student loan. You do not have to include in your income an amount of a student loan that is cancelled because, under the terms of the loan, you work for a certain period of time in a designated profession for any of a broad class of employers. However, to qualify for this exclusion, the loan must be from the government, certain public benefit corporations, or from a specified educational organization.

Example. You receive a student loan from your state government to help you attend medical school. Under the terms of the loan, the amount you owe will be cancelled if, after you graduate and receive your medical license, you work as a

61

physician for at least 2 years in a medically-underserved area of the state. You fulfill these terms of the loan, and the outstanding debt is cancelled. You do not include the cancelled amount in your income.

Cancellation of deductible debt. You do not realize income from debt cancellation to the extent that payment of the debt would have given rise to a deduction.

Example. You use the cash method of accounting for your business. You obtain business accounting services on credit. Later, when you are having trouble paying your business debts, although you are not bankrupt or insolvent, your accountant forgives part of the amount you owe for the accounting services. You do not include the amount of the debt cancellation in income, because payment for the services would have been deductible as a business expense under your method of accounting.

However, if, in the above example, you use the accrual method of accounting, your accountant's cancellation of your debt must be included in your income. This is so because, under the accrual method of accounting, the expense is deductible when the liability is incurred, not when the debt is paid. For information on the cash and accrual methods of accounting, see Publication 538, *Accounting Periods and Methods.*

Excluded cancellations. In spite of the general rule requiring inclusion of a cancelled debt in gross income, you do not include a cancelled debt in gross income if *any* of the following situations apply:

1) The cancellation takes place in a bankruptcy case under title 11 of the United States Code (the Bankruptcy Code).

2) The cancellation takes place when you are insolvent (see *Insolvency,* later), and the amount excluded is not more than the amount by which you are insolvent.

3) The cancelled debt is *qualified farm debt,* which is discussed later.

Order of exclusions. If you have debt cancelled because of a title 11 bankruptcy case, and you are insolvent and/or have qualified farm debt, the exclusion for title 11 bankruptcy cases applies.

If you are insolvent and have qualified farm debt and you have debt cancelled, the exclusion for insolvent taxpayers applies to the extent you are insolvent.

If you are neither insolvent nor in a title 11 bankruptcy case, but you do have qualified farm debt, the exclusion for qualified farm debt applies if such debt is cancelled.

Bankruptcy

Bankruptcy case exclusion. For this purpose, a bankruptcy case is a case under title 11 of the

United States Code, provided that you are under the jurisdiction of the court and the discharge of the debt is granted by the court or occurs as a result of a plan approved by the court and carried out by you.

None of the debt cancelled in a bankruptcy case is included in your gross income in the year cancelled. Instead, you must use the amount cancelled to reduce certain of your *tax attributes.* See *Reduction of Tax Attributes,* later. You may choose to first reduce the basis of depreciable property by the amount of debt cancelled before reducing other tax attributes. This is also discussed later.

Insolvency

Insolvency exclusion. You are insolvent when, and to the extent, your liabilities exceed the fair market value of your assets. For any discharge of debt, you must determine your liabilities and the fair market value of your assets immediately before the discharge to determine whether or not you are insolvent and the amount by which you are insolvent.

You exclude from your gross income debt cancelled when you are insolvent, but only up to the amount by which you are insolvent. You must use the amount excluded, however, to reduce certain tax attributes, as explained later under *Reduction of Tax Attributes.* But in reducing tax attributes, you may choose to first reduce the basis of depreciable property, as discussed later.

Example. $4,000 of the Simpson Corporation's liabilities are cancelled outside bankruptcy. Immediately before the cancellation, the Simpson Corporation's liabilities totalled $21,000 and the fair market value of its assets was $17,500. Since its liabilities were more than its assets, it was insolvent. The amount of the insolvency was $3,500 ($21,000 − $17,500).

The corporation may exclude only $3,500 of the $4,000 debt cancellation from income because that is the amount by which it was insolvent. The remaining $500 of cancelled debt must be included in income.

Farm Debts

Qualified farm debt exclusion. Even if you are solvent, you can exclude from your gross income a cancellation or discharge of *qualified farm debt* if the debt is discharged by a *qualified person.*

Qualified farm debt. Your debt is qualified farm debt if:

1) You incurred the debt directly in your operation of a farming business, and

2) At least 50% of your total gross receipts for the 3 years preceding the tax year of the debt cancellation were from farming.

Qualified person. The person that cancels or forgives your qualified farm debt is a qualified person if that person is actively and regularly engaged in the business of lending money and is not—

1) Related to you,
2) A person from whom you acquired the property securing the debt or a person related to that person, or
3) A person who received a fee in connection with your investment in the property securing the debt or a person related to that person.

The term "qualified person" includes any federal, state, or local government (or any agency or instrumentality of those governments).

Exclusion limit. The amount excluded because of the cancellation of qualified farm debt cannot exceed the sum of your adjusted "tax attributes" for the tax year that your debt was cancelled and the total adjusted basis of your "qualified property" as of the beginning of the tax year following the tax year that your debt was cancelled.

This limit is figured after any tax attribute reductions you make because of debt cancellations you were granted when you were insolvent.

Tax attributes for this purpose are:

• Net operating losses,
• General business credit carryovers,
• Capital losses,
• Foreign tax credit carryovers.

To figure your *adjusted tax attributes* you must adjust your credit attributes to make them more comparable to your deduction attributes. You do this by multiplying the dollar amount of your general business credits and your foreign tax credits by 3.

For example, if you have a general business credit carryover of $100, you must multiply that amount by 3 to figure the amount properly includible in the sum of your adjusted tax attributes. Thus, instead of adding $100 to your other tax attributes, if any, you would add $300.

Qualified property is any of your property that you use or hold for use in a trade or business (business property) or for the production of income (investment property).

Reduction of Tax Attributes

If you exclude cancelled debt from income because it is cancelled in a bankruptcy case or during insolvency, or because the debt that is cancelled is qualified farm debt, you must use the excluded amount to reduce certain of your "tax attributes." Tax attributes, for this purpose, include "basis" of certain assets as well as those attributes listed earlier. By reducing these tax attributes, tax on the cancelled debt is in part postponed instead of being entirely forgiven. This prevents an excessive tax benefit from the debt cancellation.

Order of reduction. Generally, you must use the amount of cancelled debt to reduce the tax attributes in the following order. However, you may choose to use all or a portion of the amount of cancelled debt to first reduce the basis of your depreciable property before reducing the other tax attributes. This choice is discussed later.

Net operating loss. First, reduce any net operating loss for the tax year in which the debt cancellation takes place, and any net operating loss carryover to that tax year.

General business credit carryovers. Second, reduce any carryovers, to or from the tax year of the debt cancellation, of amounts used to determine the general business credit.

Capital losses. Third, reduce any net capital loss for the tax year of the debt cancellation, and any capital loss carryover to that year.

Basis. Fourth, reduce the basis of your property as described under *Basis Reduction,* later. This reduction applies to the basis of both depreciable and nondepreciable property.

Foreign tax credit. Last, reduce any carryover, to or from the tax year of the debt cancellation, of an amount used to determine the foreign tax credit or the Puerto Rico and possession tax credit.

Amount of reduction. Except for the credit carryovers, you reduce the tax attributes listed earlier one dollar for each dollar of cancelled debt that is excluded from income. You reduce the credit carryovers by 33⅓ cents for each dollar of cancelled debt that is excluded from income.

Making the reduction. You make the required reductions in tax attributes after figuring the tax for the tax year of the debt cancellation. In reducing net operating losses and capital losses, first reduce the loss for the tax year of the debt cancellation, and then any loss carryovers to that year in the order of the tax years from which the carryovers arose, starting with the earliest year. Make the reductions of credit carryovers in the order in which the carryovers are taken into account for the tax year of the debt cancellation.

Individuals' tax attributes. If you are an individual filing for bankruptcy under chapter 7 (liquidation) or chapter 11 (reorganization) of title 11 of the United States Code, the required reduction of tax attributes must be made to the attributes acquired by the bankruptcy estate, a separate taxable entity resulting from the filing of the case. Also, the choice of whether to first reduce the basis of depreciable property before reducing other tax attributes must be made by the trustee of the bankruptcy estate. See the discussion of *Individuals' Bankruptcy Estates,* later.

Basis Reduction

If any amount of your debt cancellation is used to reduce the basis of your assets as discussed under *Reduction of Tax Attributes,* the following rules apply to the extent indicated.

When to make the basis reduction. You make the reduction in basis at the beginning of the tax year following the tax year of the debt cancellation. The reduction applies to property that you hold at that time.

Bankruptcy and insolvency reduction limit. The reduction in basis because of cancelled debt in bankruptcy or in insolvency cannot be more than the total basis of property you held immediately after the debt cancellation, minus your total liabilities immediately after the cancellation. This limit does not apply if you elect to reduce basis before reducing other attributes. This election is discussed later.

Exempt property. If your debt is cancelled in a bankruptcy case under title 11 of the United States Code, you make no reduction in basis for property that you treat as exempt property under section 522 of title 11.

Special rules for qualified farm debt. If you are a solvent farmer and exclude from your income a cancellation of qualified farm debt, you must use the excluded amount to reduce the basis of your *qualified property* only.

Qualified property is any of your property that you use or hold for your use in a trade or business (business property) or for the production of income (investment property).

Order of reduction. You must reduce the basis of your qualified property in the following order:

1) Depreciable property.
2) Land you use or hold for your use in farming.
3) Other qualified property.

Election to reduce basis first. You may choose to reduce the basis of depreciable property before reducing any other tax attributes. However, this reduction of the basis of depreciable property cannot exceed the total basis of depreciable property that you held at the beginning of the tax year following the tax year of your debt cancellation.

Depreciable property, for this purpose, means any property subject to depreciation, but only if a reduction of basis will reduce the amount of depreciation or amortization otherwise allowable for the period immediately following the basis reduction.

Real property inventory. You may choose to treat as depreciable property, for this purpose, any real property that is stock in trade or is held primarily for sale to customers in the ordinary course of trade or business. You must generally make this choice on the tax return for the tax year of the debt cancellation, and, once made, you can only revoke it with I.R.S. approval. However, if you establish reasonable cause, you may make the choice with an amended return or claim for refund or credit.

Making elections. You make the choice to reduce the basis of depreciable property before reducing other tax attributes as well as the choice to treat real property inventory as depreciable property, on Form 982, *Reduction of Tax Attributes Due to Discharge of Indebtedness.*

Recapture of basis reductions. If property, the basis of which is reduced under these provisions, is later sold or otherwise disposed of at a gain, the part of the gain that is attributable to this basis reduction is taxable as ordinary income. You figure the ordinary income part by treating the amount of this basis reduction as a depreciation deduction and by treating any such basis-reduced property that is not already either section 1245 or section 1250 property as section 1245 property. In the case of section 1250 property, you make the determination of what would have been straight line depreciation as though there had been no basis reduction for debt cancellation. Sections 1245 and 1250 and the recapture of gain as ordinary income are explained in *Chapter 4, Dispositions of Depreciable Property,* in Publication 544, *Sales and Other Dispositions of Assets.*

Example of Tax Attribute Reduction

The sample filled-in Form 982, *Reduction of Tax Attributes Due to Discharge of Indebtedness,* shown in this publication is based on the following situation.

Tom Smith is in financial difficulty, but he has been able to avoid declaring bankruptcy. This year, he reached an agreement with his creditors, whereby they agreed to forgive $10,000 of the total that he owed them, in return for his setting up a schedule for repayment of the rest of his debts.

Immediately before the debt cancellation, Tom's liabilities totalled $120,000 and the fair market value of his assets was $100,000 (his total basis in all these assets was $90,000). At the time of the debt cancellation, therefore, he was insolvent by $20,000. He can exclude from income the entire $10,000 debt cancellation since it was not more than the amount by which he was insolvent.

Among Tom's assets, the only depreciable asset is a rental condominium with an adjusted basis of $50,000. Of this, $10,000 is allocable to the land, leaving a depreciable basis of $40,000. During the tax year of the debt discharge, Tom had a net capital loss of $5,000 resulting from sales of stock at a loss. He also has a net operating loss carryover to this year of $3,000 from a previous tax year.

Tom's adjusted gross income for the year, without considering the discharge of debt, the capital loss, or the net operating loss carryover, is $20,000. He does not itemize deductions, and he has no general business credit or foreign tax credit arising in the year of the debt discharge or carried to this year.

Form **982**	**Reduction of Tax Attributes Due to Discharge of Indebtedness** (Also, Section 1082 Basis Adjustment)	OMB No. 1545-0046 Expires 11-30-89
(Rev. December 1986) Department of the Treasury Internal Revenue Service	▶ Attach this form to your income tax return.	Attachment Sequence No. **51**

Name *Tom Smith*	Identifying number (SSN or EIN) *000-00-0000*

Part I   General Information

1 Amount excluded is due to (check applicable box(es)):
a Discharge of indebtedness in a title 11 case . . . . ☐
b Discharge of indebtedness to the extent insolvent (not in a title 11 case) . . . . . . ☒
c Discharge of "qualified business indebtedness" occurring before January 1, 1987 (not in a title 11 case nor to the extent the taxpayer is insolvent) . . . . ☐
d Discharge of "qualified farm indebtedness" (See instructions for line 1d before completing Part II) . . . . ☐

2 Total amount of discharged indebtedness excluded from gross income . . . . **2** | *$10,000*

3 Do you elect to treat all real property described in section 1221(1), relating to property held for sale to customers in the ordinary course of a trade or business, as if it were depreciable property? . . . . ☐ Yes ☒ No

Part II   Reduction of Tax Attributes
Note: *You must attach a description of the transactions resulting in the reduction in basis under section 1017.*

Enter amount excluded from gross income:

4 Under 1a and/or 1b which you elect to apply first to reduce the basis (under section 1017) of depreciable property	**4**	*$10,000*
5 Applied to reduce any net operating loss which occurred in the tax year of the discharge or carried over to the tax year of the discharge.	**5**	
6 Applied to reduce certain credit carryovers comprising the general business credit to or from the tax year of the discharge	**6**	
7 Applied to reduce any net capital loss for the taxable year of the discharge including any capital loss carryovers to the tax year of discharge	**7**	
8 Applied to reduce the basis of nondepreciable assets and depreciable assets if not reduced on line 4 except in the case of discharge of qualified farm indebtedness	**8**	
9 Applied to reduce any carryover to or from the taxable year of the discharge for determining the foreign tax credit	**9**	
10 Which you elect to treat as qualified business indebtedness and apply to reduce the basis of depreciable property	**10**	
11 For discharge of qualified farm indebtedness, applied to reduce the basis of property other than the basis of land used or held for use in the trade or business of farming	**11**	
12 For discharge of qualified farm indebtedness, applied to reduce the basis of land used or held for use in the trade or business of farming	**12**	

Part III   Consent of Corporation to Adjustment of Basis of its Property Under Section 1082(a)(2) of the Internal Revenue Code

The corporation named above has excluded under section 1081(b) of the Internal Revenue Code $ . . . .

from its gross income for the tax year beginning . . . . , and ending . . . .
Under that section the corporation consents to have the basis of its property adjusted in accordance with the regulations prescribed under section 1082(a)(2) of the Internal Revenue Code in effect at the time of filing its income tax return for that year. The corporation is

organized under the laws of . . . .
(State of incorporation)

Note: *You must attach a description of the transactions resulting in the nonrecognition of gain under section 1081.*

Signature

Under penalties of perjury, I declare that I have examined this form, including accompanying schedules and statements, and to the best of my knowledge and belief, it is true, correct, and complete

. . . . *Tom Smith* . . . . *4-10-88* . . . . . .
(Signature—if individual taxpayer)   (Date)

. . . .
(Signature of officer—if corporate taxpayer)   (Title)   (Date)

For Paperwork Reduction Act Notice, see back of form.   Form **982** (Rev 12-86)

Ordinarily, in applying the $10,000 debt discharge amount to reduce tax attributes, Tom would first eliminate his $3,000 net operating loss carryover, and then his $5,000 net capital loss. He would then have $2,000 remaining to apply to basis reduction, but would not have to reduce basis because his total basis in assets ($90,000) was less than his total liabilities, immediately after the debt cancellation ($120,000 − $10,000 = $110,000).

However, Tom figures that it is better for him to preserve his current deductions of $3,000 for the net operating loss carryover and $3,000 for the net capital loss, plus the $2,000 capital loss carryover ($5,000 − $3,000) to the following year. (Only $3,000 of a net capital loss can be applied to offset other income in any one tax year.) He can do this by choosing to reduce the basis of his depreciable property before making other tax attribute reductions.

Tom elects to reduce basis first. Therefore, Tom can reduce the depreciable basis of his rental condominium (his only depreciable asset) by $10,000. The tax effect of doing this will be to reduce Tom's depreciation deductions for years following the year of the debt cancellation. However, if Tom later sells the condominium at a gain, the part of the gain attributable to the basis reduction will be taxable as ordinary income.

Tom must file Form 982, as shown here, with his individual return (Form 1040) for the tax year of the debt discharge. In addition, he must attach a statement describing the debt cancellation transaction and identifying the property to which the basis reduction applies. This statement is not illustrated.

Individuals' Bankruptcy Estates

If you are an individual debtor who files for bankruptcy under chapter 7 or 11 of the Bankruptcy Code, a separate "estate" is created consisting of property that belonged to you before the filing date. This bankruptcy estate is a new taxable entity, completely separate from you as an individual taxpayer. The estate is represented by a trustee (or a **debtor in possession** in a chapter 11 case, unless a trustee is appointed) who manages the estate for the benefit of any creditors. The estate may produce its own income as well as incur its own expenses. The creation of a separate bankruptcy estate also gives you a "fresh start" —with certain exceptions, wages you earn and property you acquire after the bankruptcy case has begun belong to you and do not become a part of the bankruptcy estate.

A separate estate is not created for a corporation or a partnership. Nor is a separate estate created for an individual who files for bankruptcy under chapter 12 or 13. The bankruptcy estate can only be created if you are an individual who has begun bankruptcy proceedings based on liquidation (chapter 7) or reorganization (chapter 11). However, if you own a partnership interest, it is treated in the same way as any of your other property.

If your bankruptcy case was begun but is later dismissed by the bankruptcy court, the estate is not treated as a separate entity, and you are treated as if the bankruptcy petition had never been filed in the first place. For the effects of such dismissals on your filing requirements, see the later discussion of return requirements.

Choice to End Tax Year

If you are an individual debtor and have assets other than those that you may treat as exempt property, you may choose to end your tax year on the day before the filing of your bankruptcy case. Once you make this choice, you may not change it. If you make the choice, your tax year is divided into two "short" tax years of less than 12 months each. The first year ends on the day before the filing date, and the second year begins with the filing date and ends on the date your tax year normally ends.

Once you make the choice, your income tax liability for the first short tax year becomes an allowable claim (as a claim arising before bankruptcy) against the bankruptcy estate. Any tax liability for that year is collectible from the estate as long as enough assets are available to pay off the estate's debts. However, to the extent that assets of the bankruptcy estate are not enough to pay any tax due for that year, the remaining liability is not dischargeable in the bankruptcy case, and can be collected from you as an individual taxpayer after the case. If you do not choose to end the tax year, then no part of your tax liability for the year in which bankruptcy proceedings begin can be collected from the estate.

Choice by debtor's spouse. If you are married, your spouse may also join in the choice to end the tax year, but only if you and your spouse file a joint return for the first short tax year. You must make these choices by the due date for filing the return for the first short tax year. Once you make the choice, it cannot be revoked for the first year; however, the choice does not mean that you and your spouse must file a joint return for the second short tax year.

Making the choice. If you choose to end your tax year you do so by filing a return on Form 1040 for the first short tax year on or before the 15th day of the fourth full month after the end of that first tax year. To avoid delays in processing the return, you should write "Section 1398 Election" at the top of the return. You may also make the choice by attaching a statement to that effect to an application for extension of time to file a tax return (Form 4868 or other). You must file the application for extension by the due date of the return for the first short tax year. The statement must say that you choose under section 1398(d)(2) to close your tax year on the day before the filing of the bankruptcy case. If your spouse decides to also close his or her tax year, he or she must file a joint return with you for the first short tax year. He or she must also join in any application for extension and attached statement.

Later bankruptcy of spouse.   If your spouse files for bankruptcy later in the same year, he or she may also choose to end his or her tax year, regardless of whether he or she joined in the choice to end your tax year. Because each of you has a separate bankruptcy, one or both of you may have three short tax years in the same calendar year. If your spouse had joined in your choice, or if you had not made the choice to end your tax year, you can join in your spouse's choice. But if you had made a choice and your spouse had decided not to join in the choice, you cannot join in your spouse's later choice. This is because you and your spouse, having different tax years, could not file a joint return for a year ending on the day before your spouse's filing of bankruptcy.

Example 1.   Paul and Mary Harris are calendar-year taxpayers. A voluntary chapter 7 bankruptcy case involving only Paul begins on March 4.

If Paul does not make a choice, his tax year does not end on March 3. If he does make a choice, Paul's first tax year is January 1—March 3, and his second short tax year begins on March 4. Mary could join in Paul's choice as long as they file a joint return for the tax year January 1—March 3. They must make the choice on or before July 15, the due date for filing the joint return.

Example 2.   Fred and Ethel Barnes are calendar-year taxpayers. A voluntary chapter 7 bankruptcy case involving only Fred begins on May 6, and a bankruptcy case involving only Ethel begins on November 1 of the same year.

Ethel could choose to end her tax year on October 31. If Fred had not chosen to end his tax year on May 5, or if he had chosen to do so but Ethel had not joined in his choice, Ethel would have two tax years in the same calendar year if she decided to close her tax year. Her first tax year is January 1—October 31, and her second year is November 1—December 31.

If Fred had not decided to end his tax year as of May 5, he could join in Ethel's choice to close her tax year on October 31, but only if they file a joint return for the tax year January 1—October 31. If Fred had chosen to end his tax year on May 5, but Ethel had not joined in Fred's choice, Fred could not join in Ethel's choice to end her tax year on October 31, because they could not file a joint return for that short year. They could not file a joint return because their tax years preceding October 31 were not the same.

Example 3.   Jack and Karen Thomas are calendar-year taxpayers. A voluntary chapter 7 bankruptcy case involving only Jack begins on April 10, and a voluntary chapter 7 bankruptcy case involving only Karen begins on October 3 of the same year. Jack chooses to close his tax year on April 9 and Karen joins in Jack's choice.

Under these facts, Karen would have three tax years for the same calendar year if she makes the choice relating to her own bankruptcy case. The first tax year would be January 1—April 9; the second April 10—October 2; and the third October 3—December 31.

Jack may (but does not have to) join in Karen's choice if they file a joint return for the second short tax year (April 10—October 2). If Jack does join in, he would have the same three short tax years as Karen. Also, if Jack joins in Karen's choice, they may file a joint return for the third tax year (October 3—December 31), but they are not required to do so.

Annualizing taxable income.   If you choose to close your tax year, you must annualize your taxable income for each short tax year in the same way that is done for a change in an annual accounting period. For information on this, see *Short Tax Year* in Publication 538, *Accounting Periods and Methods.*

Treatment of Income, Deductions, and Credits

The gross income of your bankruptcy estate includes any of your gross income to which the estate is entitled under the bankruptcy law. It does not include amounts that you receive (or accrue, if you use the accrual method of accounting) as income before the beginning of the bankruptcy case. However, the estate, not you as an individual taxpayer, must include any gross income the estate is entitled to and receives or accrues after the beginning of the bankruptcy case.

The bankruptcy estate may deduct or take as a credit any expenses it pays or incurs, in the same way that you would have deducted or credited them had you continued in the same trade, business, or activity and actually paid or accrued the expenses. Allowable expenses include administrative expenses, such as attorney fees and court costs.

The taxable income of the bankruptcy estate is figured in the same way as for an individual. The estate, in arriving at its taxable income, is allowed one personal exemption, individual deductions, and, if it does not itemize deductions, the basic standard deduction that would be allowed for a married individual filing separately. The tax on the taxable income is figured by using the rates for a married individual filing separately. The tax, if any, will be paid by the trustee or by the debtor in possession.

Transfers Between Debtor and Estate

A transfer (other than by sale or exchange) of an asset from you to the bankruptcy estate is not treated as a "disposition" for income tax purposes. This means that the transfer does not result in gain or loss, recapture of deductions or credits, or acceleration of income or deductions. For example, the transfer of an installment obligation to the estate would not accelerate gain under the rules for reporting installment sales. The estate is treated just as you would be with respect to the transferred asset.

When the bankruptcy estate is terminated, that is, dissolved, any resulting transfer (other than by sale or exchange) of the estate's assets back to you is not treated as a disposition. Therefore, as with the transfer of an asset to the estate, discussed above, this transfer does not result in gain or loss, recapture of deductions or credits, or acceleration of income or deductions. You are treated in the same way the estate would be regarding the transferred assets.

Attribute Carryovers

The bankruptcy estate must treat its tax attributes, discussed earlier, in the same way that you would have treated them as the individual debtor. These items must be determined as of the first day of your tax year in which your bankruptcy case begins. The bankruptcy estate gets the following items from you:

1) Net operating loss carryovers.
2) Carryovers of excess charitable contributions.
3) Recovery of tax benefit items.
4) Credit carryovers.
5) Capital loss carryovers.
6) Basis, holding period, and character of assets.
7) Method of accounting (the same as you use).
8) Other tax attributes as provided in regulations.

Termination of the estate. If the bankruptcy estate has any tax attributes at the time it is terminated, you must assume the attributes and treat them in the same way the estate treated them. You must assume these attributes even if they first arose during the administration of the estate.

Administration Expenses

The bankruptcy estate is allowed a deduction for administrative expenses and any fees or charges assessed against it under chapter 123 of title 28 of the United States Code. These expenses are deductible whether or not they are considered trade or business expenses or investment expenses. However, such expenses are subject to disallowance under other provisions of the Internal Revenue Code, such as the provisions disallowing certain capital expenditures, taxes, or expenses relating to tax-exempt interest. Those expenses belonging to, or directly related to, the estate can only be deducted by the estate, and never by you, the debtor.

If the administrative expenses of the bankruptcy estate are more than its gross income for the tax year, the excess amount may be carried back three years or forward seven years. The amounts can only be carried back or forward to a tax year of the estate and never to your tax year as the individual taxpayer. The excess amount to be carried back or forward is treated like a net operating loss and must first be carried back to the earliest year possible. For a discussion of the net operating loss, see Publication 536, *Net Operating Losses*.

Other Special Rules

Change of accounting period. The bankruptcy estate may change its accounting period, that is, its tax year, once without getting approval from the Internal Revenue Service. This rule allows the trustee of the estate to close the estate's tax year early; that is, before the expected termination of the estate. The trustee can then file a return for the first short tax year to get a quick determination of the estate's tax liability.

Carrybacks from the estate. If the bankruptcy estate itself has a net operating loss, apart from any losses passing to the estate from you as the individual debtor, it can carry the loss back not only to its own earlier tax years, but also to your tax years before the year in which the bankruptcy case began. The estate may also carry back excess credits, such as the general business credit, to your pre-bankruptcy years.

Carrybacks from your activities. You, as the individual debtor, cannot carry back any net operating loss or credit carryback from a tax year ending after the bankruptcy case has begun to any tax year ending before the case began. The estate, however, can carry the loss back to offset your pre-bankruptcy income.

Return Requirements and Payment of Tax

If the gross income of a chapter 7 or 11 bankruptcy estate of an individual is at least the following amounts, the trustee in bankruptcy must file a federal income tax return on Form 1041, *U.S. Fiduciary Income Tax Return,* for the year.

For tax years beginning in:	Return required if gross income is at least:
1987	$3,780
1988	$4,450
1989	$4,500

For tax years beginning after 1989, the filing requirement will be adjusted for inflation.

To avoid confusion with the individual debtor's short year return, the trustee should show the name, address, employer identification number, tax year, and tax liability of the bankruptcy estate on Form 1041. The trustee must sign it and attach a Form 1040, *U.S. Individual Income Tax Return,* to it as a supporting schedule showing the income, deductions, credits, etc., of the estate.

The trustee in bankruptcy is responsible for obtaining an employer identification number for the estate for use in filing any tax returns, including estimated tax returns. This number is obtained by filing a Form SS–4, *Application for Employer Identification Number,* available from I.R.S. offices. Trustees representing ten or more estates (other than estates that will be filing employment or excise tax returns) may file a consolidated application for employer identification (ID) numbers or may obtain blocks of ten or more employer ID numbers by following the procedures set out in Revenue Procedure 70–22, 1970–2 C.B. 503.

Caution: The trustee (or debtor in possession) must withhold income and social security taxes and file employment tax returns with respect to any wages paid by the trustee (or debtor), including wage claims paid as administrative expenses. Until these employment taxes are deposited as required by the Internal Revenue Code, they should be set apart in a separate bank account to ensure that funds are available to satisfy the liability. If the employment taxes are not paid as required, the trustee may be held personally liable for payment of the taxes.

The trustee has the duty to prepare and file Forms W–2, *Wage and Tax Statement,* in connection with wage claims paid by the trustee, regardless of whether the claims accrued before or during bankruptcy. If the debtor fails to prepare and file Forms W–2 for wages paid before bankruptcy, the trustee should instruct the employees to file an IRS Form 4852, *Employee's Substitute Wage and Tax Statement,* with their individual income tax returns.

You, as an individual debtor, must generally also file a return for the tax year on Form 1040. If you make the choice to end your tax year on the day before filing the bankruptcy case, you must file the return for the first short tax year as explained earlier.

If the bankruptcy case is later dismissed or converted to a chapter 12 or 13 case, you should inform the I.R.S. of that fact by notifying the Service Center where you filed the short year Form 1040. In this situation, you must recompute the tax because no separate bankruptcy estate is created. You must file an amended return to replace any return filed by the bankruptcy estate and any full or short year returns that you filed.

If you choose to end your tax year, you must also file a separate Form 1040 for the second

short tax year by the regular due date. You should note on the return that it is the "Second Short Year Return After Section 1398 Election."

Disclosure of return information. If you have filed for bankruptcy under chapter 7 or 11 of title 11, whether or not the bankruptcy case is later dismissed, your income tax returns for the year the bankruptcy case begins and for earlier years are, upon written request, open to inspection by or disclosure to the trustee. If the bankruptcy case was not voluntary, disclosure cannot be made before the bankruptcy court has entered an order for relief, unless the court rules that the disclosure is needed for determining whether relief should be ordered.

In bankruptcy cases, other than those of individuals filing under chapter 7 or 11, and in receivership proceedings where substantially all the debtor's property is in the hands of the receiver, current and earlier returns of the debtor are also, upon written request, open to inspection by or disclosure to the trustee or receiver, but only if the Internal Revenue Service finds that the trustee or receiver has a material interest which will be affected by information contained in the returns.

The bankruptcy estate's income tax returns are open, upon written request, to inspection by or disclosure to you the individual debtor. The disclosure is necessary so that you can properly figure the amount and nature of the tax attributes, if any, that you must assume when the bankruptcy estate is terminated.

Partnerships

If a partnership's debt is cancelled because of bankruptcy or insolvency, or if its qualified farm debt is cancelled, the rules for exclusion of the cancelled amount from gross income and for tax attribute reduction are applied at the individual partner level. This means that all choices, such as the choices to reduce the basis of depreciable property before reducing other tax attributes, to treat real property inventory as depreciable property, and to end the tax year on the day before filing the bankruptcy case, must be made by the individual partners, not the partnership.

Depreciable property. For purposes of reducing the basis of depreciable property in attribute reduction, a partnership interest of a partner is treated as depreciable property to the extent of the partner's proportionate interest in the partnership's depreciable property. This applies only if the partnership makes a corresponding reduction in the partnership's basis in its depreciable property with respect to the partner.

Partner's basis in partnership. The allocation of an amount of debt discharge income to a partner results in that partner's basis in the partnership being increased by that amount. At the same time, the reduction in the partner's share of partnership liabilities caused by the debt discharge results in a deemed distribution, in turn resulting in a reduction of the partner's basis in the partnership. These basis adjustments are separate from any basis reduction under the attribute-reduction rules described earlier.

Filing requirements. The filing requirements for a partnership in bankruptcy proceedings do not change. However, the filing of required returns may become the responsibility of an appointed trustee, receiver, or a debtor in possession, rather than a general partner.

Corporations

The following discussion covers only the highlights of the bankruptcy tax rules applying to corporations. Because the details of corporate bankruptcy reorganizations are beyond the scope of this publication, you may wish to refer such issues to a professional tax advisor.

Equity-for-Debt Rules

Generally, if a corporation issues its own stock to a creditor in exchange for the cancellation of its debt, the corporation realizes debt cancellation income to the extent that the amount of debt cancelled exceeds the fair market value of the stock.

Exception for bankruptcy or insolvency. Generally, a corporation does not realize income (or have to reduce its tax attributes) because of such stock for debt exchanges if it is in bankruptcy, or to the extent it is insolvent.

De minimis exception. However, a corporation that is in bankruptcy or is insolvent will have a debt discharge amount that may be subject to inclusion in gross income or to attribute reduction if it issues only nominal or token shares in exchange for the cancellation of its debt. Also, the corporation will have a debt discharge amount that is subject to inclusion in gross income (or attribute reduction) with respect to an unsecured creditor in a workout, if the value of stock received by the creditor in exchange for cancellation of the debt is less than half the value of stock that the creditor would receive if all the corporation's unsecured creditors taking part in the workout received a pro-rata amount of the stock issued. A "workout" includes a title 11 bankruptcy case or other transaction or series of transactions involving a significant restructuring of the debt of a corporation in financial difficulty. These two debt discharge amounts are subject to the rules discussed earlier under *Cancellation or Forgiveness of Your Debt* relating to inclusion in gross income, attribute reduction, etc.

Example 1. Mr. Smith, a creditor, held $1,000 of unsecured debt against a debtor corporation. In a title 11 bankruptcy case workout, the corporation fully satisfied $10,000 of its unsecured debt by the transfer of $6,000 (60% of the debt cancelled) of its stock to creditors. Mr. Smith must receive at least $300 ($1,000 × 60% = $600 ×50%) of stock in satisfaction of his claim in order for the debtor corporation to rely on the rule that it has no debt discharge amount with respect to the cancellation of Mr. Smith's claim in exchange for stock. If Mr. Smith receives only $100 of stock for his $1,000 debt, then the debtor corporation will have a debt discharge amount of $900 with respect to Mr. Smith. Because the corporation is in bankruptcy, it does not include the $900 in income. However, it must reduce its tax attributes, if any, by the $900 amount.

Example 2. The facts are the same as in Example 1, except that the corporation is not bankrupt or insolvent. In this case, regardless of the value of the stock Mr. Smith receives in satisfaction of the debt, the corporation realizes debt cancellation income with respect to Mr. Smith's claim equal to the difference between the $1,000 debt and the fair market value of the stock transferred to him.

Recapture of gain on later sale. If a creditor receives stock of a debtor corporation in satisfaction of the corporation's debt, the stock, and any other property the basis of which is determined by reference to the adjusted basis of the stock, is treated as section 1245 property (discussed earlier, and fully explained in Publication 544). For purposes of section 1245, the total amount allowed to the creditor as a bad debt deduction or as an ordinary loss on the exchange, reduced by any amount included in the creditor's gross income on the exchange, is considered an amount allowed as a depreciation deduction. This means that a gain on the later sale of the stock by the creditor is ordinary income to the extent of the creditor's bad debt deduction or ordinary loss.

In an exchange of the stock in a section 354, 355, or 356 tax-free reorganization (described later), the amount of gain treated as ordinary income under this rule is limited to the gain recognized in the tax-free reorganization.

Debt contributed to capital. If a debtor corporation's shareholder cancels a debt the corporation owes to the shareholder as a contribution to capital, the corporation realizes a debt discharge amount only to the extent that the amount of debt cancelled exceeds the shareholder's adjusted basis in the indebtedness.

Example. An accrual-basis corporation accrues and deducts, but does not actually pay, a $1,000 liability to a shareholder-employee as salary. The shareholder-employee is on the cash basis and so does not include the $1,000 in income. In a later year, the shareholder-employee forgives the debt as a contribution of capital. In this situation, the corporation has a debt discharge amount of $1,000, the amount of debt cancelled ($1,000) that exceeds the shareholder's adjusted basis in the debt (zero). If the corporation is insolvent or in bankruptcy, it must apply the $1,000 debt discharge amount to reduce tax attributes, as explained earlier. If the corporation is solvent and outside bankruptcy, it must include the $1,000 in income in the year of the debt cancellation.

On the other hand, if the shareholder-employee is on the accrual basis and includes the salary in income when accrued, the shareholder's basis in the debt is $1,000. At the time of the cancellation, the corporation has no debt discharge amount, and no inclusion in income or tax attribute reduction is required.

Tax-Free Reorganizations

The tax-free reorganization provisions of the Internal Revenue Code apply to a transfer by a corporation of all or part of its assets to another corporation in a title 11 or similar case, but only if, under the reorganization plan, stock or securities of the corporation to which the assets are transferred are distributed in a transaction which qualifies under section 354, 355, or 356 of the Code.

A "title 11 or similar case," for this purpose, is a bankruptcy case under title 11 of the United States Code, or a receivership, foreclosure, or similar proceeding in a federal or state court, but only if the corporation is under the jurisdiction of the court in the case and the transfer of assets is under a plan of reorganization approved by the court. In a receivership, foreclosure, or similar proceeding before a federal or state agency involving certain financial institutions, the agency is treated as a court.

Generally, section 354 of the Internal Revenue Code provides that no gain or loss is recognized if a corporation's stock is exchanged solely for stock or securities in the same or another corporation under a qualifying reorganization plan. Thus, under section 354, shareholders in the bankrupt corporation would recognize no gain or loss if they exchange their stock solely for stock or securities of the corporation acquiring the bankrupt's assets.

Section 355 generally provides that no gain or loss is recognized by a shareholder if a corporation distributes solely stock or securities of another corporation that the distributing corporation controls immediately before the distribution. Section 356 provides that in an exchange that would qualify under section 354 or 355 except that other property or money besides the permitted stock or securities is received by the shareholder, gain is recognized by the shareholder only to the extent of the money and the fair market value of the other property received. No loss is recognized in this situation.

Earnings and Profits

The earnings and profits of a corporation do not include income from the discharge of indebtedness to the extent of the amount applied to reduce the basis of the corporation's property as explained earlier in this publication. Otherwise,

discharge of indebtedness income, including amounts excluded from gross income, increases the earnings and profits of the corporation (or reduces a deficit in earnings and profits).

If there is a deficit in the earnings and profits of a corporation and the interest of any shareholder of the corporation is terminated or extinguished in a title 11 or similar case (defined earlier), the deficit must be reduced by an amount equal to the paid-in capital allocable to the shareholder's terminated or extinguished interest.

Filing Requirements

The filing requirements of a corporation involved in bankruptcy proceedings do not change. However, the filing of required returns may become the responsibility of an appointed trustee, receiver, or a debtor in possession, rather than a corporate officer.

Exemption from tax return filing. If you are a trustee, receiver, or an assignee of a corporation that is in bankruptcy, in receivership, in dissolution, or in the hands of an assignee by court order, you may apply to your IRS District Director to be relieved from having to file federal income tax returns for the corporation. To qualify, the corporation must have ceased business operations and must have neither assets nor income.

Your request to the District Director must include the name, address, and employer identification number of the corporation, the date on which you filed the notice of qualification as fiduciary (discussed at the end of this publication), and a statement of the facts (with supporting documents, if necessary) showing why you need relief from the filing requirements. You must also include a statement that you are making the request and furnishing the information under the penalties of perjury. The District Director will act on your request within 90 days.

Personal Holding Company Tax

A corporation that is subject to the jurisdiction of the court in a title 11 or similar case is exempt from the personal holding company tax, unless a major purpose of beginning or continuing the case is the avoidance of this tax. A "title 11 or similar case" is defined earlier under *Tax-Free Reorganizations*.

S Corporations

In the case of an S corporation, the rules for excluding income from debt cancellation because of bankruptcy, insolvency, and because the debt is qualified farm debt apply at the corporate level.

Net operating losses. A loss or deduction that is disallowed for the tax year of the debt discharge, because it exceeds the shareholders' basis in the corporation's stock and debt, is nevertheless treated as a net operating loss for that tax year in making the required reduction of tax attributes for the amount of the discharged debt.

Adjustments to shareholder's basis in debt of the S corporation. If section 1367(b)(2) of the Code requires a shareholder of an S corporation to reduce the basis of debt owed to that shareholder by the S corporation, that adjustment is ignored when determining the S corporation's income from discharge of debt owed to that shareholder. However, this rule applies only if the debt cancellation is treated as a contribution of capital to the S corporation. See the earlier discussion of the special rule for *Debt contributed to capital.*

Filing requirements. See the earlier discussion under *Filing Requirements.*

Bankruptcy estate as a shareholder. A bankruptcy estate of an individual in a title 11 case may be a shareholder in a small business corporation without disqualifying the corporation from S corporation treatment. For more information on the requirements for S corporation treatment, see Publication 589, *Tax Information on S Corporations.*

Transactions Involving Related Parties

In determining the income of a debtor from the discharge of indebtedness, the acquisition of outstanding indebtedness of the debtor by a person related to the debtor from an unrelated person, generally may be treated as the acquisition of the indebtedness by the debtor. This rule is intended to treat a debtor as having debt discharged if a party related to the debtor purchases the debt at a discount, for example, where a parent corporation purchases at a discount debt issued by its subsidiary.

Related persons. For this purpose, the following persons are considered related:

1) An individual and the individual's spouse, children, grandchildren, parents, or any spouse of the individual's children or grandchildren,

2) An individual and a corporation more than 50 percent in value of the outstanding stock of which is owned, directly or indirectly, by or for that individual,

3) Two corporations or other business entities that are under common control,

4) A grantor and a fiduciary of a trust,

5) A fiduciary and a beneficiary of a trust,

6) A fiduciary of a trust and a fiduciary of another trust, if the same person is a grantor of both trusts,

7) A fiduciary of a trust and a beneficiary of another trust, if the same person is a grantor of both trusts,

8) A fiduciary of a trust and a corporation more than 50 percent in value of the outstanding stock of which is owned, directly or indirectly, by or for the trust or by or for a grantor of the trust,

9) A person and a tax-exempt organization controlled directly or indirectly by that person or, if the person is an individual, by members of that person's family,

10) A corporation and a partnership if the same persons own more more than 50 percent in value of the outstanding stock of the corporation and more than 50 percent of the capital or profits interests in the partnership,

11) An S corporation and another corporation (S or C) if the same persons own more than 50 percent in value of the outstanding stock of each corporation,

12) A partnership and a partner owning, directly or indirectly, more than 50 percent of the capital or profits interest in the partnership, and

13) Two partnerships in which the same persons own, directly or indirectly, more than 50 percent of the capital or profits interests.

Tax Procedures

The following section discusses the procedures for determining the amount of tax due from you or your bankruptcy estate, paying the tax claim, and obtaining a discharge of the tax liability.

Determination of Tax

The first step in obtaining a determination of the tax due is filing a return. As an individual bankrupt debtor, you file a Form 1040 for the tax year involved, and the trustee of your bankruptcy estate files a Form 1041, as explained earlier under *Individuals' Bankruptcy Estates.* A bankrupt corporation, or a receiver, bankruptcy trustee, or assignee having possession of, or holding title to, substantially all the property or business of the corporation, files a Form 1120 for the tax year.

Note: Interest on trust accounts in Chapter 13 proceedings. If you are an individual debtor in a Chapter 13 wage earner's plan, do not include as income on your return interest earned on amounts held in trust accounts while awaiting distribution to your creditors. This interest is not available either to you or to your creditors. It is available only to the trustees, and is, therefore, taxable to them as their individual income.

After the return is filed, the Internal Revenue Service may redetermine the tax liability shown on the return. When the administrative remedies within the Service have been exhausted, the tax issue may be litigated either in the bankruptcy court or in the U.S. Tax Court, as explained in the following discussion.

Bankruptcy court jurisdiction. Generally, the bankruptcy court has authority to determine the amount or legality of any tax imposed on the debtor or the estate, including any fine, penalty, or addition to tax, whether or not the tax was previously assessed or paid.

The bankruptcy court does not have authority to determine the amount or legality of a tax, fine, penalty, or addition to tax that was contested before and finally decided by a court or administrative tribunal of competent jurisdiction (that became *res judicata*) before the date of filing the bankruptcy petition.

Also, the bankruptcy court does not have authority to decide the right of the bankruptcy estate to a tax refund until the trustee of the estate properly requests the refund from the Internal Revenue Service and either the Service determines the refund or 120 days pass after the date of the request.

If you as the debtor have already claimed a refund or credit for an overpayment of tax on a properly filed return or claim for refund, the trustee may rely on that claim. Otherwise, if the credit or refund was not claimed by you, the trustee may make the request by filing the appropriate original or amended return or form with the District Director for the district in which the bankruptcy case is pending. The return or claim for refund should be marked "For the personal attention of the special procedures function. Do not open in mailroom."

The appropriate form for the trustee to use in making the claim for refund is as follows:

1) For income taxes for which you as the individual debtor had filed a Form 1040, Form 1040A, or Form 1040EZ, the trustee should use a Form 1040X, *Amended U.S. Individual Income Tax Return.*

2) For income taxes for which a corporate debtor had filed a Form 1120, the trustee should use a Form 1120X, *Amended U.S. Corporation Income Tax Return.*

3) For income taxes for which a debtor had filed a form other than Form 1040, Form 1040A, Form 1040EZ, or Form 1120, the trustee should use the same type of form that the debtor had originally filed, marking the form "Amended Return" at the top.

4) For taxes other than income taxes for which the debtor had filed a return, the trustee should use a Form 843, *Claim,* attaching an exact copy of any return that is the subject of the claim along with a statement of the name and location of the office where the return was filed.

5) For overpayment of taxes of the bankruptcy estate incurred during the administration of the case, the trustee may choose to use a properly executed tax return (for income taxes, a Form 1041) as a claim for refund or credit.

The I.R.S. Examination Function, if requested by the trustee or debtor in possession as discussed later, will examine the appropriate amended return, claim, or original return filed by the trustee on an expedite basis, and will complete the examination and notify the trustee of its decision within 120 days from the date of filing of the claim.

Tax Court jurisdiction. The filing of a bankruptcy petition automatically results in a stay (suspension) of any U.S. Tax Court proceeding to determine your tax liability as the debtor. This stay continues until one of the acts removing it occurs. The stay may be lifted by the bankruptcy court upon your request, the request of the IRS, or the request of any other party in interest. Since the bankruptcy court has power to lift the stay and allow you to begin or continue a Tax Court case involving your tax liability, the bankruptcy court has, in effect, during the pendency of the stay, the sole authority to determine whether the tax issue is decided in the bankruptcy court itself or in the Tax Court.

The bankruptcy court could lift the stay if you seek to litigate in the Tax Court and the trustee wishes to intervene in that proceeding. In that case, the merits of the tax controversy may be determined by the Tax Court.

Suspension of time for filing. In any bankruptcy case, the 90–day period for filing a Tax Court petition, after the issuance of the statutory notice of deficiency, is suspended for the time you are prevented from filing the petition because of the bankruptcy case, and for 60 days thereafter. However, even if the statutory notice was issued before the bankruptcy petition was filed, the suspension exists if any part of the 90–day period remained at the date the bankruptcy petition was filed.

Trustee may intervene. The trustee of your bankruptcy estate in any title 11 bankruptcy case may intervene, on behalf of the estate, in any proceeding in the U.S. Tax Court to which you are a party.

Assessment of tax. After the determination of a tax by either the bankruptcy court or the U.S. Tax Court, the Internal Revenue Service may assess the tax against the estate, or against you or your successor, subject to applicable law.

Immediate assessments. In bankruptcy situations, the Internal Revenue Service has limited authority to immediately assess tax deficiencies, without following the normal procedure under which it issues a deficiency notice. However, you can challenge the tax liability asserted under that authority in the U.S. Tax Court without payment of tax. In a title 11 bankruptcy case, an immediate assessment of tax may be made for a tax liability incurred by the debtor's estate, or on you, provided the liability for the tax has been finally decided (has become *res judicata*) in the bankruptcy case. No purpose would be served by requiring issuance of a deficiency notice prior to assessment of taxes imposed on the bankruptcy estate, or on you when the liability has been finally determined in the bankruptcy court, because in neither case can the issue be litigated in the Tax Court.

Statute of limitations for assessment. In a title 11 bankruptcy case, the period of limitations for assessment of tax (generally, 3 years after the later of the date the return was due or was filed) is suspended for the period during which the Internal Revenue Service is prohibited, because of the bankruptcy case, from making the assessment, plus 60 days thereafter.

Payment of Tax Claim

After the filing of a bankruptcy petition and during the period your assets or those of the bankruptcy estate are under the jurisdiction of the bankruptcy court, these assets are not subject to levy. To collect these taxes, the Internal Revenue Service must file a proof of claim in the bankruptcy court, in the same way as other creditors. This claim may be presented to the bankruptcy court even though the taxes have not yet been assessed or are subject to a Tax Court proceeding.

Seventh priority taxes. In bankruptcy, your debts are assigned priorities for payment. Most of your prepetition tax debts are classified as seventh priority claims. Generally, *prepetition taxes* are certain of your income and other taxes that are considered owed before you file your petition for bankruptcy protection.

The following federal taxes, if unsecured, are prepetition seventh priority taxes of the government:

1) Income taxes for tax years ending on or before the date of filing the bankruptcy petition, for which a return is last due (including extensions) after a date three years before the filing of the petition.

2) Income taxes assessed within 240 days before the date of filing the petition. This 240-day period is increased by any time, plus 30 days, during which an offer in compromise with respect to these taxes was pending, that was made within 240 days after the assessment.

3) Income taxes, other than those for which no return, a late return (filed within two years of the filing of the bankruptcy petition), or a fraudulent return was filed, that were not assessed before but were assessable as of the date of the filing of the petition.

4) Withholding taxes for which you are liable in any capacity.

5) Employment taxes on the first $2,000 of wages, salaries, or commissions (including vacation, severance, and sick leave pay) earned by each individual employee from the debtor within the 90-day period before the earlier of the date of cessation of your business or the date of filing the bankruptcy petition (whether or not actually paid before that date), for which a return is last due (including extensions) after a date three years before the filing of the petition.

6) Excise taxes on transactions occurring before the date of filing the bankruptcy petition, for which a return, if required, is last due (including extensions) after a date three years before the filing of the petition. If a return is not required, these excise taxes include only those on transactions occurring during the three years immediately before the date of filing the petition.

Priority of payment. If a proper and timely proof of claim was filed by the Internal Revenue Service, the preceding seventh priority prepetition taxes may be paid out of the assets of the bankruptcy estate, to the extent that there are assets remaining after paying the claims of secured creditors and those other creditors having higher priority claims.

Certain taxes are assigned a higher priority for payment. Taxes assessed during administration by the bankruptcy estate are paid first, as administrative expenses. Taxes arising in the ordinary course of your business or financial affairs in an *involuntary* bankruptcy case, after the filing of the bankruptcy petition but before the earlier of the appointment of a trustee or the order for relief are included in the second priority of payment. The employee's portion of the employment taxes on the first $2,000 described in (5) above is included in the third priority.

Relief from penalties. A penalty for failure to pay tax, including failure to pay estimated tax, will not be imposed with respect to the period during which a title 11 bankruptcy case is pending, under the following conditions. If the tax was incurred by the bankruptcy estate, the penalty will not be imposed if the failure to pay resulted from an order of the court finding probable insufficiency of funds of the estate to pay administrative expenses. If the tax was incurred by you as the debtor, the penalty will not be imposed if: (1) the tax was incurred before the earlier of the order for relief or (in an involuntary case) the appointment of a trustee, and (2) the bankruptcy petition was filed before the due date for the tax return (including extensions) or the date for imposing the penalty occurs on or after the day the bankruptcy petition was filed.

This relief from the failure-to-pay penalty does not apply to any penalty for failure to pay or deposit tax withheld or collected from others and required to be paid over to the U.S. government.

Nor does it apply to any penalty for failure to timely file a return.

Preservation of FUTA credit. An employer is generally allowed a credit against the federal unemployment tax (FUTA tax) for contributions made to a state unemployment fund, provided the contributions are paid by the last day for filing an unemployment tax return for the tax year. If the contributions to the state fund are paid after that date, generally only 90% of the otherwise allowable credit may be taken against the federal unemployment tax.

However, for any unemployment tax on wages paid by the trustee of a title 11 bankruptcy estate, if the failure to pay the state unemployment contributions on time was without fault by the trustee, the full amount of the credit is allowed.

Discharge of Unpaid Tax

As a general rule, there is *no discharge* for you as an individual debtor at the termination of a bankruptcy case for the second and seventh priority taxes described earlier, or for taxes for which no return, a late return (filed after a date two years before the filing of the bankruptcy petition), or a fraudulent return was filed. *However,* claims against you for other taxes predating the bankruptcy petition by more than 3 years *may be discharged.*

Exception for individuals with regular income. If you complete all payments under a chapter 13 debt adjustment plan for an individual with regular income, the court may grant you a discharge of debts, *including* a discharge of the second and seventh priority prepetition taxes described earlier. However, if you fail to complete all payments under the plan, these taxes are not discharged although the court may grant a discharge of other debts in limited circumstances.

Discharge of bankruptcy estate's tax liability. The trustee of the bankruptcy estate may request a determination of any unpaid liability of the estate for tax incurred *during the administration of the case* by the filing a tax return and a request for such a determination with the Internal Revenue Service. Unless the return is fraudulent or contains a material misrepresentation, the trustee, you as the debtor, and any successor to you are discharged from liability for the tax upon payment of the tax:

1) As determined by the Internal Revenue Service,

2) As determined by the bankruptcy court, after the completion of the I.R.S. examination, or

3) As shown on the return, provided the I.R.S. does not: (a) notify the trustee within 60 days

after the request for the determination that the return has been selected for examination, or (b) complete the examination and notify the trustee of any tax due within 180 days after the request (or any additional time permitted by the bankruptcy court).

Making the request for determination. To request a prompt determination of any unpaid tax liability of the estate, the trustee must file a written application for the determination with the I.R.S. District Director for the district in which the bankruptcy case is pending. The application must be submitted in duplicate and executed under the penalties of perjury. The trustee must submit with the application an exact copy of the return (or returns) filed by the trustee with the I.R.S. for a completed tax period, and a statement of the name and location of the office where the return was filed. The envelope should be marked "For the personal attention of the special procedures function. Do not open in mailroom."

The I.R.S. Examination Function will notify the trustee within 60 days from receipt of the application whether the return filed by the trustee has been selected for examination or has been accepted as filed. If the return is selected for examination, it will be examined as soon as possible. The Examination Function will notify the trustee of any tax due within 180 days from receipt of the application or within any additional time permitted by the bankruptcy court.

Notice of qualification as fiduciary. Every receiver, assignee for benefit of creditors, or similar fiduciary (other than a fiduciary in a bankruptcy case appointed, qualified, or authorized to act after January 28, 1988), must give notice of his or her qualification as such to the Internal Revenue Service within 10 days of appointment or authorization to act. The period of limitations for assessment of tax is extended by the time from the institution of the receivership or other proceeding to a date 30 days after the notice of qualification is received by the I.R.S. However, this extension cannot be for more than 2 years.

The notice of qualification must be in writing and must be filed with the District Director for the district in which the debtor files tax returns. It should be marked for the attention of the special procedures staff. The notice must contain the following information:

1) The name, address, and date of appointment of the receiver or other fiduciary,

2) The name, address, and taxpayer identifying number of the debtor,

3) The name and location of the court in which the proceedings are pending,

4) The date on which the proceedings were instituted, and the docket number, and

5) When possible, the date, time, and place of any hearing, meeting of creditors, or other scheduled action in the proceedings.

This notice is not required of bankruptcy trustees, debtors in possession, or other like fiduciaries in bankruptcy cases, for appointments, qualifications, and authorizations to act made after January 28, 1988. However, notice to the Treasury Department may still be required under the Bankruptcy Rules.

Statute of limitations for collection. In a title 11 bankruptcy case, the period of limitations for collection of tax (generally, 6 years after assessment) is suspended for the period during which the Internal Revenue Service is prohibited from assessing or collecting, plus 6 months thereafter.

Index

APPENDIX II

BANKRUPTCY FORMS

FIRST STEPS

PROCEEDINGS

Notice to Creditors of Automatic Stay   Form that debtor's attorney sends to creditors of the debtor announcing the commencement of the Automatic stay   94

Notice of Commencement of Case   Announcement sent to creditors listed on debtor's matrix (alphabetical listing of creditors) following voluntary bankruptcy filing:

SCHEDULES

Summary of Schedules   Summary sheet for assets, and other listings on Schedules A through J   98

Schedule A—Real Property   Form for listing of real property description and location, nature of interest in property, current market value, and amount of secured claim   99

Schedule B—Personal Property   Form for listing type of property (cash, security deposits, household furnishings, books, pictures, clothing, furs, jewelry, firearms, insurance policy interests, etc.) with description, location, and current market value   100

Schedule C—Property Claimed as Exempt   Form allowing debtor to elect exemptions (federal, state, local), with description, basis for exemption claim, value   101

Schedule D—Creditors Holding Secured Claims   Form for listing creditor names and addresses, date and amount of claim, unsecured portion   102

Schedule E—Creditors Holding Unsecured Priority Claims   Form for listing creditor names and addresses, date and amount claimed, priority amount   103

Schedule F—Creditors Holding Unsecured Nonpriority Claims   Form for listing creditor names and addresses, date and amount claimed   107

Schedule G—Executory Contracts and Unexpired Leases   Forms for listing names and addresses of parties to leases or contracts, with descriptions   112

Schedule H—Codebtors   Form for listing names and addresses of codebtors/guarantors and relevant creditors   113

Schedule I—Current Income of Individual Debtor(s)   Form for Chapter 12 or 13 filing by individual or a married couple, with details about income sources and amounts   114

CREDITORS' ACTIONS

FOLLOW-UP ACTIONS

PRELIMINARY QUESTIONNAIRE

In re _____)
)   PRELIMINARY
)   QUESTIONNAIRE
)
_____ Debtor   )

   This questionnaire has been designed to organize information to expedite the proceedings on your file. Please assist us by typing or printing legibly. The answers to Part A, 1., should be entered in the appropriate places on the enclosed worksheet, and the answers to A, 2. through 5., should be entered directly after the question. The documents referred to in Part B should be checked off and brought with you to our office.

PART A

   1. DEBTS:— List debts with an exact full name, address, zip code, year debt was incurred, balance due and basis of debt. *Please use attached sheet for this purpose and print clearly.*

   2. MONIES DUE TO YOU:— Print the name, address, zip code and basis of debts due to you with the present balance owed for each person or firm owing money to you. Writings establishing your claim to these monies should be brought to our office.

Name and address of persons or firms owing money to you include zip code	Is their a writing evidencing this claim? (Yes or No)	Present balance owed to you
1.		
2.		
3.		

   3. LOANS REPAID:— If any loans were repaid by you during the last year, please print (for each lender) the name and address of the lender, the original amount borrowed, the date the loan was received, the amount and dates of repayment and if the lender was a relative.

Name and address of lender	Original amount borrowed	Date loan received	Amount and dates of repayment	Was lender a relative?
1.				
2.				
3.				
4.				
5.				

Please complete reverse side

PRELIMINARY QUESTIONNAIRE (Continued)

4. SECURED CREDITORS:— If any creditor is holding any security on your property (for example, mortgage, lien, security interest, deposits for rent or utilities), please furnish the name and address of these creditors, the nature of the security, the amount of the deposit and furnish the attorney with a copy of any documents evidencing the security.

Name and address of secured creditor	Nature of the security Mortgage, Lien, security interest (auto or other personal property), pledge, pawn deposit for rent or utilities, etc.	Amount of deposit, if any?
1.		
2.		
3.		
4.		
5.		

5. TAX REFUND:— Did you receive a tax refund last year? ☐ No   ☐ Yes, amount $............................

Are you entitled to any other refunds? ☐ No   ☐ Yes, amount $............................

PART B

The following documents should be brought to our office:

☐ All correspondence received from collection agencies and attorneys.

☐ Guarantees and notes signed as principal, endorser or comaker.

☐ Deed to real property, if any.

☐ Insurance policies.

☐ Summonses, complaints and judgments.

☐ Savings books of both open and closed accounts maintained over the past two years.

☐ Checkbooks maintained over the past two years.

☐ Documents establishing claims to money due to you (referred in Part A. 2, above).

☐ Documents evidencing security (referred to in Part A, 4, above).

T 1057—Questionnaire and checklist for client.   ©1975 Julius Blumberg, Inc.

DEBTOR'S WORKSHEET

LIST OF DEBTS — PRINT OR TYPE

Name & Address of Creditors
Personal loans, rent, banks, finance and loan co.'s, credit cards, contracts, stores, medical, dental, car payments, and any other debt of any kind. Include street address or post office box, city, state, zip code, and name of person at creditor's business who is familiar with debt.

	Year Debt Incurred	Total Balance Due	Basis of Debt — Goods Sold and Delivered, Work, Labor and Services, Loan, Guarantee, etc.	I have papers covering debt.	I dispute this debt.	Legal action started on this debt.	Office use only
1							A-1 ☐ A-2 ☐ A-3 ☐
2							A-1 ☐ A-2 ☐ A-3 ☐
3							A-1 ☐ A-2 ☐ A-3 ☐
4							A-1 ☐ A-2 ☐ A-3 ☐
5							A-1 ☐ A-2 ☐ A-3 ☐
6							A-1 ☐ A-2 ☐ A-3 ☐
7							A-1 ☐ A-2 ☐ A-3 ☐
8							A-1 ☐ A-2 ☐ A-3 ☐
9							A-1 ☐ A-2 ☐ A-3 ☐
10							A-1 ☐ A-2 ☐ A-3 ☐
11							A-1 ☐ A-2 ☐ A-3 ☐
12							A-1 ☐ A-2 ☐ A-3 ☐
13							A-1 ☐ A-2 ☐ A-3 ☐
14							A-1 ☐ A-2 ☐ A-3 ☐
15							A-1 ☐ A-2 ☐ A-3 ☐

Enter "yes" in appropriate columns.

SAMPLE

Forms may be purchased from Julius Blumberg, Inc., NYC 10013, or any of its dealers. Reproduction prohibited.

83

DEBTOR'S WORKSHEET (Continued)

LIST OF DEBTS — PRINT OR TYPE

Name & Address of Creditors — Personal loans, rent, banks, finance and loan co.'s, credit cards, contracts, stores, medical, dental, car payments, and any other debt of any kind. Include street address or post office box, city, state, zip code, and name of person at creditor's business who is familiar with debt.	Year Debt Incurred	Total Balance Due	Basis of Debt — Goods Sold and Delivered Work, Labor and Services Loan, Guarantee, etc.	Enter "yes" in appropriate columns.			Office use only
				I have papers covering debt.	I dispute this debt.	Legal action started on this debt.	
16							A-1 ☐ A-2 ☐ A-3 ☐
17							A-1 ☐ A-2 ☐ A-3 ☐
18							A-1 ☐ A-2 ☐ A-3 ☐
19							A-1 ☐ A-2 ☐ A-3 ☐
20							A-1 ☐ A-2 ☐ A-3 ☐
21							A-1 ☐ A-2 ☐ A-3 ☐
22							A-1 ☐ A-2 ☐ A-3 ☐
23							A-1 ☐ A-2 ☐ A-3 ☐
24							A-1 ☐ A-2 ☐ A-3 ☐
25							A-1 ☐ A-2 ☐ A-3 ☐
26							A-1 ☐ A-2 ☐ A-3 ☐
27							A-1 ☐ A-2 ☐ A-3 ☐
28							A-1 ☐ A-2 ☐ A-3 ☐
29							A-1 ☐ A-2 ☐ A-3 ☐
30							A-1 ☐ A-2 ☐ A-3 ☐

SAMPLE

Forms may be purchased from Julius Blumberg, Inc., NYC 10013, or any of its dealers. Reproduction prohibited.

84

VOLUNTARY PETITION

Blumberg Law Products

Form 1, P1 (6-90)

Julius Blumberg, Inc. NYC 10013

FORM 1 VOLUNTARY PETITION

United States Bankruptcy Court	VOLUNTARY PETITION
District of	

IN RE (Name of debtor-If individual, enter Last, First, Middle)	NAME OF JOINT DEBTOR (Spouse) (Last, First, Middle)
ALL OTHER NAMES used by debtor in the last 6 years (Include married, maiden and trade names)	ALL OTHER NAMES used by the joint debtor in the last 6 years (Include married, maiden and trade names.)
SOC. SEC./TAX I.D. NO. (If more than one, state all)	SOC. SEC./TAX I.D. NO.(If more than one, state all)
STREET ADDRESS OF DEBTOR (No. and street, city, state, zip)	STREET ADDRESS OF JOINT DEBTOR (No. and street, city, state, zip)
COUNTY OF RESIDENCE OR PRINCIPAL PLACE OF BUSINESS	COUNTY OF RESIDENCE OR PRINCIPAL PLACE OF BUSINESS
MAILING ADDRESS OF DEBTOR (If different from street address)	MAILING ADDRESS OF JOINT DEBTOR (If different from street address)

LOCATION OF PRINCIPAL ASSETS OF BUSINESS DEBTOR (If different from addresses listed above)	☐ Debtor has been domiciled or has had a residence, principal place of business or principal assets in this District for 180 days immediately preceding the date of this petition or for a longer part of such 180 days than in any other District. ☐ There is a bankruptcy case concerning debtor's affiliate, general partner or partnership pending in this District.

INFORMATION REGARDING DEBTOR (Check applicable boxes)

TYPE OF DEBTOR		CHAPTER OR SECTION OF BANKRUPTCY CODE UNDER WHICH THE PETITION IS FILED (Check one box)
☐ Individual	☐ Corporation Publicly Held	
☐ Joint (H&W)	☐ Corporation Not Publicly Held	☐ Chapter 7 ☐ Chapter 11 ☐ Chapter 13
☐ Partnership	☐ Municipality	☐ Chapter 9 ☐ Chapter 12 ☐ § 304-Case Ancillary to Foreign Proceeding
☐ Other _____		FILING FEE (Check one box)

NATURE OF DEBT
☐ Non-Business Consumer ☐ Business - Complete A & B below

☐ Filing fee attached.
☐ Filing fee to be paid in installments. (Applicable to individuals only) Must attach signed application for the court's consideration certifying that the debtor is unable to pay fee except in installments. Rule 1006(b). see Offical Form No..3

A. TYPE OF BUSINESS (check one box)

☐ Farming	☐ Transportation	☐ Commodity Broker
☐ Professional	☐ Manufacturing Mining	☒ Construction
☐ Retail/Wholesale		☐ Real Estate
☐ Railroad	☐ Stockbroker	☐ Other Business

NAME AND ADDRESS OF LAW FIRM OR ATTORNEY

B. BRIEFLY DESCRIBE NATURE OF BUSINESS

Telephone No.

NAME(S) OF ATTORNEY(S) DESIGNATED TO REPRESENT THE DEBTOR

☐ Debtor is not represented by an attorney

STATISTICAL ADMINISTRATIVE INFORMATION (28 U.S.C. § 604) (Estimates only) (Check applicable boxes)	THIS SPACE FOR COURT USE ONLY

☐ Debtor estimates that funds will be available for distribution to unsecured creditors.
☐ Debtor estimates that after any exempt property is excluded and administrative expenses paid, there will be no funds available for distribution to unsecured creditors.

ESTIMATED NUMBER OF CREDITORS
☐ 1-15 ☐ 16-49 ☐ 50-99 ☐ 100-199 ☐ 200-999 ☐ 1000-over

ESTIMATED ASSETS (in thousands of dollars)
☐ Under 50 ☐ 50-99 ☐ 100-499 ☐ 500-999 ☐ 1000-9999 ☐ 10,000-99,000 ☐ over 100,000

ESTIMATED LIABILITIES (in thousands of dollars)
☐ Under 50 ☐ 50-99 ☐ 100-499 ☐ 500-999 ☐ 1000-9999 ☐ 10,000-99,000 ☐ over 100,000

ESTIMATED NUMBER OF EMPLOYEES -CH 11 & 12 ONLY
☐ 0 ☐ 1-19 ☐ 20-99 ☐ 100-999 ☐ 1000-over

ESTIMATED NO . OF EQUITY SECURITY HOLDERS - CH 11 & 12 ONLY
☐ 0 ☐ 1-19 ☐ 20-99 ☐ 100-499 ☐ 500-over

3050-1© 1991 JULIUS BLUMBERG, INC., NYC 10013

VOLUNTARY PETITION (Continued)

Form 1, P2 (6-90) Julius Blumberg, Inc. NYC 10013

Name of Debtor _____ Case No. _____

(Court use only)

FILING OF PLAN

For Chapter 9, 11,12 and13 cases only. Check appropriate box.

☐ A copy of debtor's proposed plan dated _____ is attached.

☐ Debtor intends to file a plan within the time allowed by statute, rule, or order of the court.

PRIOR BANKRUPTCY CASE FILED WITHIN LAST 6 YEARS (If more than one, attach additional sheet)

Location Where Filed	Case Number	Date Filed

PENDING BANKRUPTCY CASE FILED BY ANY SPOUSE, PARTNER, OR AFFILIATE OF THIS DEBTOR (if more than one, attach additional sheet.)

Name of Debtor	Case Number	Date
Relationship	District	Judge

REQUEST FOR RELIEF

Debtor requests relief in accordance with the chapter of title II, United States Code, specified in this petition.

SIGNATURES

ATTORNEY

X _____   Date _____
Signature

INDIVIDUAL /JOINT DEBTOR(S)	CORPORATE OR PARTNERSHIP DEBTOR
I declare under penalty of perjury that the information provided in this petition is true and correct.	I declare under penalty of perjury that the information provided in this petition is true and correct, and that the filing of this petition on behalf of the debtor has been authorized.
X _____ Signature of Debtor Date	X _____ Signature of Authorized Individual
	Print or Type Name of Authorized Individual
X _____ Signature of Joint Debtor Date	Title of Individual Authorized by Debtor to File this Petition Date

EXHIBIT "A" (To be completed if debtor is a corporation requesting relief under chapter 11.)

☐ Exhibit "A" is attached and made a part of this petition.

TO BE COMPLETED BY INDIVIDUAL CHAPTER 7 DEBTOR WITH PRIMARILY CONSUMER DEBTS (See P.L. 98-353 § 322)

I am aware that I may proceed under chapter 7,11,12 or 13 of title 11, United States Code, understand the relief available under each such chapter, and choose to proceed under chapter 7 of such title.

If I am represented by an attorney, exhibit "B" has been completed.

X _____   Date _____
Signature of Debtor

X _____   Date _____
Signature of Joint Debtor

EXHIBIT "B" (To be completed by attorney for individual chapter 7 debtor(s) with primarily consumer debts.)

I, the attorney for the debtor(s) named in the foregoing petition, declare that I have informed the debtor(s) that (he, she, or they) may proceed under chapter 7, 11, 12, or 13 of title 11, United States Code, and have explained the relief available under each such chapter.

X _____   Date _____
Signature of Attorney

Forms may be purchased from Julius Blumberg, Inc., NYC 10013, or any of its dealers. Reproduction prohibited.

EXHIBIT A TO VOLUNTARY PETITION

Julius Blumberg, Inc. NYC 10013

Form B1XA (6-90)

EXHIBIT "A"

UNITED STATES BANKRUPTCY COURT   **DISTRICT OF**

In re: Debtor(s)   Case No.

                                                                     Chapter

(If debtor is a corporation filing under chapter 11 of the Code, this Exhibit "A" shall be completed and attached to the petition)

EXHIBIT "A" to Voluntary Petition

1. Debtor's employer identification number is
2. If any of debtor's securities are registered under § 12 of the Securities and Exchange Act of 1934, the SEC file number is
3. The following financial data is the latest available information and refers to debtor's condition on

   a. Total assets   .... $ Approximate
   b. Total liabilities ....   number of
                                                             holders

   Fixed, liquidated secured debt ....
   Contingent secured debt ....
   Disputed secured claims ....
   Unliquidated secured debt ....

   Fixed , liquidated unsecured debt ......
   Contingent unsecured debt ....
   Disputed unsecured claims ....
   Unliquidated unsecured debt ....

   Number of shares of preferred stock.......
   Number of shares of common stock ....

Comments, if any:

4. Brief description of debtor's business:

5. List the name of any person who directly or indirectly owns, controls or holds, with power to vote, 20% or more of the voting securities of debtor:

6. List the names of all corporations 20% or more of the outstanding voting securities of which are directly or indirectly owned, controlled, or held, with power to vote, by debtor:

INVOLUNTARY PETITION

T 1050—Involuntary petition (creditors' petition),
chapter 7 or 11, Form 5, 8-91.

 Blumbergs
Law Products

JULIUS BLUMBERG, INC.
PUBLISHER, NYC 10013

FORM B5 (6-90)

FORM 5. INVOLUNTARY PETITION

United States Bankruptcy Court _____ District of _____	INVOLUNTARY PETITION

IN RE (Name of debtor - If individual, enter: Last, First, Middle)	ALL OTHER NAMES used by debtor in the last 6 years (Include married, maiden and trade names)
SOC. SEC./TAX I.D. NO. (If more than one, state all)	

STREET ADDRESS OF DEBTOR (No. and street, city, state and zip code)	MAILING ADDRESS OF DEBTOR (If different from street address)
COUNTY OR RESIDENCE OR PRINCIPAL PLACE OF BUSINESS	

LOCATION OF PRINCIPAL ASSETS OF BUSINESS DEBTOR (If different from previously listed addresses)

CHAPTER OF BANKRUPTCY CODE UNDER WHICH PETITION IS FILED

☐ Chapter 7   ☐ Chapter 11

INFORMATION REGARDING DEBTOR (Check applicable boxes)

Petitioners believe

☐ Debts are primarily consumer debts

☐ Debts are primarily business debts (Complete sections A and B)

TYPE OF DEBTOR

☐ Individual

☐ Partnership

☐ Other

☐ Corporation Publicly Held

☐ Corporation Not Publicly Held

A. TYPE OF BUSINESS (Check one)

☐ Professional   ☐ Transportation   ☐ Commodity Broker

☐ Retail/Wholesale ☐ Manufacturing/Mining ☐ Construction

☐ Railroad   ☐ Stockbroker   ☐ Real Estate

☐ Other _____

B. BRIEFLY DESCRIBE NATURE OF BUSINESS

VENUE

☐ Debtor has been domiciled or has had a residence, principal place of business, or principal assets in the District for 180 days immediately preceding the date of this petition or for a longer part of such 180 days than in any other District.

☐ A bankruptcy case concerning debtor's affiliate, general partner or partnership is pending in this District.

PENDING BANKRUPTCY CASE FILED BY OR AGAINST ANY PARTNER OR AFFILIATE OF THIS DEBTOR (Report information for any additional cases on attached sheets.)

Name of Debtor	Case Number	Date
Relationship	District	Judge

ALLEGATIONS

(Check applicable boxes)

1. ☐ Petitioner(s) are eligible to file this petition pursuant to 11 U.S.C. §303(b).

2. ☐ The debtor is a person against whom an order for relief may be entered under title 11 of the United States Code.

3.a. ☐ The debtor is generally not paying such debtor's debts as they become due, unless such debts are the subject of a bona fide dispute;

or

b. ☐ Within 120 days preceding the filing of this petition, a custodian, other than a trustee, receiver, or agent appointed or authorized to take charge of less than substantially all of the property of the debtor for the purpose of enforcing a lien against such property, was appointed or took possession.

COURT USE ONLY

INVOLUNTARY PETITION (Continued)

Name of Debtor_____

Case No. _____

(Court use only)

TRANSFER OF CLAIM

☐ Check this box if there has been a transfer of any claim against the debtor by or to any petitioner. Attach all documents evidencing the transfer and any statements that are required under Bankruptcy Rule 1003(a).

REQUEST FOR RELIEF

Petitioner(s) request that an order for relief be entered against the debtor under the chapter of title 11, United States Code, specified in this petition.

Petitioner(s) declare under penalty of perjury that the foregoing is true and correct according to the best of their knowledge, information, and belief.

X_____   X_____
Signature of Petitioner or Representative (State title)   Signature of Attorney

_____   _____
Name of Petitioner   Name of Attorney Firm (If any)

Name and Mailing   _____   _____
Address of Individual   Address
Signing in Representative
Capacity   _____   _____
                                                              Telephone No.

X_____   X_____
Signature of Petitioner or Representative (State title)   Signature of Attorney

_____   _____
Name of Petitioner   Name of Attorney Firm (If any)

Name and Mailing   _____   _____
Address of Individual   Address
Signing in Representative
Capacity   _____   _____
                                                              Telephone No.

X_____   X_____
Signature of Petitioner or Representative (State title)   Signature of Attorney

_____   _____
Name of Petitioner   Name of Attorney Firm (If any)

Name and Mailing   _____   _____
Address of Individual   Address
Signing in Representative
Capacity   _____   _____
                                                              Telephone No.

PETITIONING CREDITORS

Name and Address of Petitioner	Nature of Claim	Amount of Claim
Name and Address of Petitioner	Nature of Claim	Amount of Claim
Name and Address of Petitioner	Nature of Claim	Amount of Claim
Note: If ther are more than three petitioners, attach additional sheets with the statement under penalty of perjury, petitioner(s) signatures under the statement and the name(s) of attorney(s) and petitioning creditor information in the format above.		Total Amount of Petitioners' Claims

_____continuation sheets attached

[Application and Order to Pay Filing Fee in Installments]

UNITED STATES BANKRUPTCY COURT

_____ **DISTRICT OF** _____

In re _____,
        Debtor

Case No. _____

Chapter _____

APPLICATION TO PAY FILING FEES IN INSTALLMENTS

In accordance with Fed. R. Bankr. P. 1006, application is made for permission to pay the filing fee on the following terms:

$_____ with the filing of the petition, and the balance of

$_____ in _____ installments, as follows:

$_____ on or before _____

$_____ on or before _____

$_____ on or before _____

$_____ on or before _____

I certify that I am unable to pay the filing fee except in installments. I further certify that I have not paid any money or transferred any property to an attorney or any other person for services in connection with this case or in connection with any other pending bankruptcy case and that I will not make any payment or transfer any property for services in connection with the case until the filing fee is paid in full.

Date: _____

_____
Applicant

_____
Address of Applicant

_____

ORDER

It is ORDERED that the debtor pay the filing fee in installments on the terms set forth in the foregoing application.

IT IS FURTHER ORDERED that until the filing fee is paid in full the debtor shall not pay, and no person shall accept, any money for services in connection with this case, and the debtor shall not relinquish, and no person shall accept, any property as payment for services in connection with this case.

BY THE COURT

Date: _____   _____

POWER OF ATTORNEY

Form B11A 6/90

UNITED STATES BANKRUPTCY COURT
_____DISTRICT OF_____

In re _____   Case No. _____
                                        Debtor
                                                  Chapter _____

POWER OF ATTORNEY

To _____   of*
                                                                            and

                          of*

GENERAL POWER OF ATTORNEY *(Form 11A)*
The undersigned claimant hereby authorizes you, or any one of you, as attorney in fact for the undersigned and with full power of substitution, to vote on any question that may be lawfully submitted to creditors of the debtor in the above-entitled case, *[if appropriate] to vote for a trustee of the estate of the debtor and for a committee of creditors; to receive dividends; and in general to perform any act not constituting the practice of law for the undersigned in all matters arising in this case.*

Dated: Signed: ....
                          [If appropriate] By ....
                                            as ....
                                      Address: ....
                                                ....

* State mailing address

ACKNOWLEDGMENT

STATE OF   COUNTY OF   ss.:
     [If executed by an individual] Acknowledged before me on

     [If executed on behalf of a partnership] Acknowledged before me on
by   who says that he [or she] is a member of the partnership named
above and is authorized to execute this power of attorney in its behalf.

     [If executed on behalf of a corporation] Acknowledged before me on
by   who says that he [or she] is   of
the corporation named above and is authorized to execute this power of attorney in its behalf.

....
                                                              [Official character]

No. ....

United States Bankruptcy Court

.........DISTRICT OF

In Bankruptcy

IN THE MATTER OF

Debtor

**Proof of Claim
and
Power of Attorney**

AMOUNT OF CLAIM $ ....

(NAME)

(ADDRESS)

JULIUS BLUMBERG, INC. · NEW YORK CITY 10013

POWER OF ATTORNEY (Continued)

T 232—General and Special Powers of Attorney.
Official Forms 11A & 11B, 8-91

Blumbergs
Law Products

JULIUS BLUMBERG, INC.
PUBLISHER, NYC 10013

Form B11A 6/90 & B11B 6/90

UNITED STATES BANKRUPTCY COURT
_____DISTRICT OF_____

In re _____   Case No. _____
                                                    Debtor

                                                    Chapter _____

POWER OF ATTORNEY

To

    of*

                                                                                and

    of*

☐ **GENERAL POWER OF ATTORNEY** *(Form 11A)*
The undersigned claimant hereby authorizes you, or any one of you, as attorney in fact for the undersigned and with full power of substitution, to vote on any question that may be lawfully submitted to creditors of the debtor in the above-entitled case, [*if appropriate*] *to vote for a trustee of the estate of the debtor and for a committee of creditors; to receive dividends; and in general to perform any act not constituting the practice of law for the undersigned in all matters arising in this case.*

☐ **SPECIAL POWER OF ATTORNEY** *(Form 11B)*
The undersigned claimant hereby authorizes you, or any one of you, as attorney in fact for the undersigned [*if desired:* and with full power of substitution,] to attend the meeting of creditors of the debtor or any adjournment thereof, and to vote in my behalf on any question that may be lawfully submitted to creditors at such meeting or adjourned meeting, and for a trustee or trustees of the estate of the debtor.

    Dated:

                                    Signed: ....
                        [*If appropriate*] By ....
                                        as ....
                                    Address ....
                                            ....

_____
* State mailing address

ACKNOWLEDGMENT

STATE OF   COUNTY OF   ss.:

    [*If executed by an individual*] Acknowledged before me on

    [*If executed on behalf of a partnership*] Acknowledged before me on
by   who says that he [or she] is a member of the partnership named
above and is authorized to execute this power of attorney in its behalf.

    [*If executed on behalf of a corporation*] Acknowledged before me on
by   who says that he [or she] is   of the corporation
named above and is authorized to execute this power of attorney in its behalf.

                                    ....

                                    ....
                                            [*Official character*]

ATTORNEY'S COMPENSATION

3085   Statement of compensation: Rule 2016(b), 8-91

Blumbergs
Law Products

UNITED STATES BANKRUPTCY COURT   **DISTRICT OF**

In re   Debtor(s)   Case No.   (If Known)

STATEMENT
Pursuant to Rule 2016(b)

The undersigned, pursuant to Rule 2016(b) Bankruptcy Rules, states that:

(1) The undersigned is the attorney for the debtor(s) in this case.

(2) The compensation paid or agreed to be paid by the debtor(s) to the undersigned is:

   (a) for legal services rendered or to be rendered in contemplation of and in connection
      with this case .... $ ....

   (b) prior to filing this statement, debtor(s) have paid .... $ ....

   (c) the unpaid balance due and payable is .... $ ....

(3) $ .... of the filing fee in this case has been paid.

(4) The services rendered or to be rendered include the following:

   (a) analysis of the financial situation, and rendering advice and assistance to the debtor(s) in determining whether to file a
      petition under title 11 of the United States Code.

   (b) preparation and filing of the petition, schedules, statement of affairs and other documents required by the court.

   (c) representation of the debtor(s) at the meeting of creditors.

(5) The source of payments made by the debtor(s) to the undersigned was from earnings, wages and compensation for services
   performed, and

(6) The source of payments to be made by the debtor(s) to the undersigned for the unpaid balance remaining, if any, will be from
   earnings, wages and compensation for services performed, and

(7) The undersigned has received no transfer, assignment or pledge of property except the following for the value stated:

(8) The undersigned has not shared or agreed to share with any other entity, other than with members of undersigned's law firm,
   any compensation paid or to be paid except as follows:

Dated: Respectfully submitted, ... *Attorney for Petitioner*

Attorney's name and address...

AUTOMATIC STAY NOTICE

Blumbergs Law Products   T 1045—Automatic stay, notice to creditors; 8-91
Typed name and address of creditor within bracket will appear through window envelope.

© 1987 BY EPHRAIM K. LEIBOWITZ, NYC
REORDER FROM JULIUS BLUMBERG, INC., NYC 10013

UNITED STATES BANKRUPTCY COURT
_____DISTRICT OF_____

In re_____

Debtor

Case No. _____

Chapter_____

┌   ┐

└   ┘

**NOTICE TO CREDITORS
OF AUTOMATIC STAY**

You are herby advised that the above Debtor has filed a petition on _____ 19____
under the following Chapter of the Bankruptcy Code, title 11, U.S.C.:

☐   7, for liquidation
☐ 11, for reorganization
☐ 12, for adjustment of debts
☐ 13, for adjustment of debts

The above case has been referred to Honorable _____
Bankruptcy Judge, who presides at

Pursuant to section 362 of the Bankruptcy Code, creditors and other legal entities, upon the filing of the said petition, are automatically stayed from:

1. Commencing or continuing judicial, administrative or other proceedings against the Debtor that was or could have been started prior to the filing of this case, or to recover a claim against the Debtor that arose before the case was filed;

2. Enforcing a judgment obtained before the petition was filed against the Debtor or the Debtor's property;

3. Attempting to obtain property of the Debtor;

4. Creating, perfecting or enforcing against property of the Debtor any lien to the extent it secures a claim that arose prior to commencement of the bankruptcy case;

5. Collecting or recovering a claim against the Debtor that arose prior to the commencement of the bankruptcy case and;

6. Setting off any debt owing to the Debtor that arose prior to the commencement of this bankruptcy case against any claim against the Debtor.

Contempt proceedings may result from a violation of the above automatic stay provided by the Bankruptcy Code.

Dated:

....
Attorney(s) for Debtor

Forms may be purchased from Julius Blumberg, Inc., NYC 10013, or any of its dealers. Reproduction prohibited.

AUTOMATIC STAY NOTICE (Continued)

No.

United States District Court

DISTRICT OF

DIVISION

IN THE MATTER OF

Debtor

NOTICE TO CREDITORS OF AUTOMATIC STAY

SAMPLE

Attorney(s) for Debtor
Office & Post Office Address & Telephone Number

JULIUS BLUMBERG, INC., NEW YORK CITY 10013

NOTICE OF COMMENCEMENT OF CASE—CHAPTER 7

FORM B9A
3/80
U S BANKRUPTCY COURT
RODINO BUILDING
970 BROAD STREET, 7TH FLOOR
NEWARK, NJ 07102-2506

United States Bankruptcy Court
DISTRICT OF NEW JERSEY

IN RE (NAME OF DEBTOR)

NOTICE OF COMMENCEMENT OF CASE
   UNDER CHAPTER 7 OF THE
   BANKRUPTCY CODE,
MEETING OF CREDITORS, AND FIXING OF DATES
   (Individual or Joint Debtor No Asset Case)

CASE NUMBER: FILED: SOC. SEC./TAX ID NOS.

                                         ADDRESS OF DEBTOR

MEETING OF CREDITORS

DATE:
HOUR:
AT:

DEBTOR'S ATTORNEY   TRUSTEE

TELEPHONE: TELEPHONE:

DEADLINE TO FILE A COMPLAINT OBJECTING TO DISCHARGE OF THE DEBTOR OR TO
   DETERMINE DISCHARGEABILITY OF CERTAIN TYPES OF DEBTS:

AT THIS TIME THERE APPEAR TO BE NO ASSETS AVAILABLE FROM WHICH PAYMENT MAY BE MADE TO UNSECURED CREDITORS. DO NOT FILE A PROOF OF CLAIM UNTIL YOU RECEIVE NOTICE TO DO SO.

COMMENCEMENT OF CASE. A petition for liquidation under chapter 7 of the Bankruptcy Code has been filed in this court by or against the person or persons named above as the debtor, and an order for relief has been entered. You will not receive notice of all documents filed in this case. All documents filed with this court, including lists of the debtor's property, debts, and property claimed as exempt are available for inspection at the office of the clerk of the bankruptcy court.

CREDITORS MAY NOT TAKE CERTAIN ACTIONS. A creditor is anyone to whom the debtor owes money or property. Under the Bankruptcy Code, the debtor is granted certain protection against creditors. Common examples of prohibited actions by creditors are contacting the debtor to demand repayment, taking action against the debtor to collect money owed to creditors or to take property of the debtor, and starting or continuing foreclosure actions, repossessions, or wage deductions. If unauthorized actions are taken by a creditor against a debtor, the court may penalize that creditor. A creditor who is considering taking action against the debtor or the property of the debtor should review section 362 of the Bankruptcy Code and may wish to seek legal advice. The staff of the clerk of the bankruptcy court is not permitted to give legal advice.

MEETING OF CREDITORS. The debtor (both husband and wife in a joint case) is required to appear at the meeting of creditors on the date and at the place set forth above for the purpose of being examined under oath. Attendance by creditors at the meeting is welcomed, but not required. At the meeting, the creditors may elect a trustee other than the one named above, elect a committee of creditors, examine the debtor, and transact such other business as may properly come before the meeting. The meeting may be continued or adjourned from time to time by notice at the meeting, without further written notice to creditors.

LIQUIDATION OF THE DEBTOR'S PROPERTY. The trustee will collect the debtor's property and turn any that is not exempt into money. At this time, however, it appears from the schedules of the debtor that there are no assets from which any distribution can be paid to creditors. If at a later date it appears that there are assets from which a distribution may be paid, the creditors will be notified and given an opportunity to file claims.

EXEMPT PROPERTY. Under state and federal law, the debtor is permitted to keep certain money or property as exempt. If a creditor believes that an exemption of money or property is not authorized by law, the creditor may file an objection. An objection must be filed not later than 30 days after the conclusion of the meeting of creditors.

DISCHARGE OF DEBTS. The debtor is seeking a discharge of debts. A discharge means that certain debts are made unenforceable against the debtor personally. Creditors whose claims against the debtor are discharged may never take action against the debtor to collect the discharged debts. If a creditor believes that the debtor should not receive any discharge of debts under section 727 of the Bankruptcy Code or that a debt owed to the creditor is not dischargeable under section 523(a)(2), (4), or (6) of the Bankruptcy Code, timely action must be taken in the bankruptcy court by the deadline set forth above labeled "Discharge of Debts." Creditors considering taking such action may wish to seek legal advice.

DO NOT FILE A PROOF OF CLAIM UNLESS YOU RECEIVE A COURT NOTICE TO DO SO

FOR THE COURT,

NOTICE OF COMMENCEMENT OF CASE—CHAPTER 13

FORM 891
6/80
U.S. BANKRUPTCY COURT
RODINO BUILDING
970 BROAD STREET, 7TH FLOOR
NEWARK, NJ 07102-2506

United States Bankruptcy Court
DISTRICT OF NEW JERSEY

**NOTICE OF COMMENCEMENT OF CASE
   UNDER CHAPTER 13 OF THE
   BANKRUPTCY CODE,
MEETING OF CREDITORS, AND FIXING OF DATES**

IN RE (NAME OF DEBTOR)

FILED: SOC. SEC./TAX ID NOS.

CASE NUMBER: ADDRESS OF DEBTOR

MEETING OF CREDITORS

DATE: NJ
HOUR:
AT:
                              FILING CLAIMS---DEADLINE TO FILE A
                              PROOF OF CLAIM

DEBTOR'S ATTORNEY   TRUSTEE

                              TELEPHONE: -   -
TELEPHONE:

CONFIRMATION HEARING
        DATE: FILING OF PLAN:

COMMENCEMENT OF CASE. An individual's debt adjustment case under chapter 13 of the Bankruptcy Code has been filed in this court by the debtor or debtors named above, and an order for relief has been entered. You will not receive notice of all documents filed in this case. All documents filed with the court, including lists of the debtor's property and debts, are available for inspection at the office of the clerk of the bankruptcy court.

CREDITORS MAY NOT TAKE CERTAIN ACTIONS. A creditor is anyone to whom the debtor owes money. Under the Bankruptcy Code, the debtor is granted certain protection against creditors. Common examples of prohibited actions by creditors are contacting the debtor to demand repayment, taking action against the debtor to collect money owed to creditors or to take property of the debtor, and starting or continuing foreclosure actions, repossessions, or wage deductions. Some protection is also given to certain codebtors of consumer debts. If unauthorized actions are taken by a creditor against a debtor, or a protected codebtor, the court may punish that creditor. A creditor who is considering taking action against the debtor or the property of the debtor, or any codebtor, should review sections 362 and 1301 of the Bankruptcy Code and may wish to seek legal advice. The staff of the clerk of the bankruptcy court is not permitted to give legal advice.

MEETING OF CREDITORS. The debtor (both husband and wife in a joint case) is required to appear at the meeting of creditors on the date and at the place set forth above labeled "Date, Time, and Location of Meeting of Creditors" for the purpose of being examined under oath. Attendance by creditors at the meeting is welcomed, but not required. At the meeting, the creditors may examine the debtor and transact such other business as may properly come before the meeting. The meeting may be continued or adjourned from time to time by notice at the meeting, without further written notice to the creditors.

PROOF OF CLAIM. Except as otherwise provided by law, in order to share in any payment from the estate, a creditor must file a proof of file claim by the date set forth above labeled "Filing Claims." The place to file the proof of claim, either in person or by mail, is the office of the clerk of the bankruptcy court. Proof of claim forms are available in the clerk's office of any bankruptcy court.

PURPOSE OF A CHAPTER 13 FILING. Chapter 13 of the Bankruptcy Code is designed to enable a debtor to pay debts in full or in part over a period of time pursuant to a plan. A plan is not effective unless approved by the bankruptcy court at a confirmation hearing. Creditors will be given notice in the event the case is dismissed or converted to another chapter of the Bankruptcy Code.

NAME	COLLATERAL	NO PAYMNT	DEFAULT TO CURE

FOR THE COURT,

SUMMARY OF SCHEDULES

 Form B6 (6-90)

Julius Blumberg, Inc. NYC 10013

UNITED STATES BANKRUPTCY COURT   **DISTRICT OF**

In re: Debtor(s)   Case No.   (If Known)

See summary below for the list of schedules. Include Unsworn Declaration under Penalty of Perjury at the end.

GENERAL INSTRUCTIONS: Schedules D, E and F have been designed for the listing of each claim only once. Even when a claim is secured only in part, or entitled to priorityonly in part, it still should be listed only once. A claim which is secured in whole or in part should be listed on Schedule D only, and a claim which is entitled to priority in whole or in part should be listed in Schedule E only. Do not list the same claim twice. If a creditor has more than one claim, such as claims arising from separate transactions, each claim should be scheduled separately.

Review the specific instructions for each schedule before completing the schedule.

SUMMARY OF SCHEDULES

Indicate as to each schedule whether that schedule is attached and state the number of pages in each. Report the totals from Schedules A, B, D, E, F, I and J in the boxes provided. Add the amounts from Schedules A and B to determine the total amount of the debtor's assets. Add the amounts from Schedules D, E, and F to determine the total amount of the debtor's liabilities.

Name of Schedule	Attached (Yes No)	Number of sheets	Amounts Scheduled		
			Assets	Liabilities	Other
A - Real Property					
B - Personal Property					
C - Property Claimed as Exempt					
D - Creditors Holding Secured Claims					
E - Creditors Holding Unsecured Priority Claims					
F - Creditors Holding Unsecured Nonpriority Claims					
G - Executory Contracts and Unexpired Leases					
H - Codebtors					
I - Current Income of Individual Debtor(s)					
J - Current Expenditures of Individual Debtor(s)					
Total Number of Sheets of All Schedules					
Total Assets					
Total Liabilities					

Forms may be purchased from Julius Blumberg, Inc., NYC 10013, or any of its dealers. Reproduction prohibited.

SCHEDULE A

Form B6 A/B, P1(6-90)   Julius Blumberg, Inc. NYC 10013

In re: Debtor(s)   Case No.   (if known)

SCHEDULE A - REAL PROPERTY

DESCRIPTION AND LOCATION OF PROPERTY	NATURE OF DEBTOR'S INTEREST IN PROPERTY	H W J C	CURRENT MARKET VALUE OF DEBTOR'S INTEREST IN PROPERTY WITHOUT DEDUCTING ANY SECURED CLAIM OR EXEMPTION	AMOUNT OF SECURED CLAIM
		Total ->	$	(Report also on Summary of Schedules.)

SCHEDULE B

Form B6B, P2 (6-90)   Julius Blumberg, Inc. NYC 10013

SCHEDULE B
PERSONAL PROPERTY

In re: Debtor(s)   Case No.   (if known)

TYPE OF PROPERTY	N O N E	DESCRIPTION AND LOCATION OF PROPERTY	H W J C	CURRENT MARKET VALUE OF DEBTOR'S INTEREST IN PROPERTY WITHOUT DEDUCTING ANY SECURED CLAIM OR EXEMPTION
10. Annuities. Itemize and name each issuer.				
11. Interests in IRA, ERISA, Keogh, or other pension or profit sharing plans. Itemize				
12. Stock and interests in incorporated and unincorporated businesses. Itemize.				
13. Interest in partnerships or joint ventures. Itemize.				
14. Government and corporate bonds and other negotiable and nonegotiable instruments.				
15. Accounts receivable.				
16. Alimony, maintenance, support, and property settlements to which the debtor is or may be entitled. Give particulars.				
17. Other liquidated debts owing debtor including tax refunds. Give particulars.				
18. Equitable or future interests, life estates, and rights or powers exercisable for the benefit of the debtor other than those listed in Schedule of Real Property.				
19. Contingent and noncontingent interests in estate of a decedent, death benefit plan, life insurance policy, or trust.				
20. Other contingent and unliquidated claims of every nature, including tax refunds, counterclaims of the debtor, and rights to setoff claims. Give estimated value of each.				
21. Patents, copyrights, and other intellectual property. Give particulars.				
22. Licenses, franchises, and other general intangibles. Give particulars.				
23. Automobiles, trucks, trailers, and other vehicles and accessories.				
24. Boats, motors, and accessories.				
25. Aircraft and accessories.				
26. Office equipment, furnishings, and supplies.				
27. Machinery, fixtures, equipment, and supplies used in business.				
28. Inventory.				
29. Animals.				
30. Crops - growing or harvested. Give particulars.				
31. Farming equipment and implements.				
32. Farm supplies, chemicals, and feed.				
33. Other personal property of any kind not already listed. Itemize.				

(Include amounts from any continuation sheets attached. Report total also on Summary of Schedules)   Total -> $

_____ continuation sheets attached

3072 © 1991 JULIUS BLUMBERG, INC., NYC 10013

SCHEDULE C

Form B6 C (6,90)   Julius Blumberg, Inc. NYC 10013

In re: Debtor(s)   Case No.   (if known)

SCHEDULE C - PROPERTY CLAIMED AS EXEMPT

Debtor elects the exemptions to which debtor is entitled under (Check one box)

☐ 11 U.S.C. § 522(b)(1): Exemptions provided in 11 U.S.C. § 522(d). Note: These exemptions are available only in certain states.

☐ 11 U.S.C. § 522(b)(2): Exemptions available under applicable nonbankruptcy federal laws, state or local law.

DESCRIPTION OF PROPERTY	SPECIFY LAW PROVIDING EACH EXEMPTION	VALUE OF CLAIMED EXEMPTION	CURRENT MARKET VALUE OF PROPERTY WITHOUT DEDUCTING EXEMPTION

SAMPLE

3072 © 1991 JULIUS BLUMBERG, INC., NYC 10013

Forms may be purchased from Julius Blumberg, Inc., NYC 10013, or any of its dealers. Reproduction prohibited.

SCHEDULE D

Form B6 D (6-90)   Julius Blumberg, Inc. NYC 10013

In re: Debtor(s)   Case No.   (if known)

SCHEDULE D - CREDITORS HOLDING SECURED CLAIMS

CREDITOR'S NAME AND MAILING ADDRESS INCLUDING ZIP CODE	CO DEBT	H W J C	DATE CLAIM WAS INCURRED, NATURE OF LIEN, AND DESCRIPTION AND MARKET VALUE OF PROPERTY SUBJECT TO LIEN	C U D	AMOUNT OF CLAIM WITHOUT DEDUCTING VALUE OF COLLATERAL	UNSECURED PORTION IF ANY
A/C #						
			VALUE $			
A/C #						
			VALUE $			
A/C #						
			VALUE $			
A/C #						
			VALUE $			
A/C #						
			VALUE $			
A/C #						
			VALUE $			
A/C #						
			VALUE $			
A/C #						
			VALUE $			
A/C #						
			VALUE $			

_____ continuation sheets attached

Subtotal -> $
(Total of this page)

Total -> $
(use only on last page)
(Report total also on Summary of Schedules)

3072 © 1991 JULIUS BLUMBERG, INC., NYC 10013

SCHEDULE E

Form B6 E (6-90)   Julius Blumberg, Inc. NYC 10013

In re: Debtor(s)   Case No.   (if known)

SCHEDULE E - CREDITORS HOLDING UNSECURED PRIORITY CLAIMS

☐ Check this box if debtor has no creditors holding unsecured priority claims to report on this Schedule E.

TYPE OF PRIORITY CLAIMS (Check the appropriate box(es) below if claims in that category are listed on the attached sheets)

☐ **Extensions of credit in an involuntary case**
Claims arising in the ordinary course of the debtor's business or financial affairs after the commencement of the case but before the earlier of the appointment of a trustee or the order for relief. 11 U.S.C § 507(a)(2).

☐ **Wages, salaries, and commissions**
Wages, salaries, and commissions, including vacation, severance, and sick leave pay owing to employees, up to a maximum of $2000 per employee, earned within 90 days immediately preceding the filing of the original petition, or the cessation of business, whichever occured first, to the extent provided in 11 U.S.C. § 507(a)(3)

☐ **Contributions to employee benefit plans**
Money owed to employee benefit plans for services rendered within 180 days immediately preceding the filing of the original petition, or the cessation of business, whichever occured first, to the extent provided in 11 U.S.C. § 507(a)(4).

☐ **Certain farmers and fishermen**
Claims of certain farmers and fishermen, up to a maximum of $2000 per farmer or fisherman, against the debtor, as provided in 11 U.S.C. § 507(a)(5).

☐ **Deposits by individuals**
Claims of individuals up to a maximum of $900 for deposits for the purchase, lease, or rental of property or services for personal, family, or household use, that were not delivered or provided. 11 U.S.C. § 507(a)(6)

☐ **Taxes and Certain Other Debts Owed to Governmental Units**
Taxes, customs duties, and penalties owing to federal, state, and local governmental units as set forth in 11 U.S.C. § 507(a)(7).

CREDITOR'S NAME AND MAILING ADDRESS INCLUDING ZIP CODE	CODEBTOR	HWJC	DATE CLAIM WAS INCURRED AND CONSIDERATION FOR CLAIM	CUD	TOTAL AMOUNT OF CLAIM	AMOUNT ENTITLED TO PRIORITY
A/C #						
A/C #						
A/C #						
A/C #						
A/C #						
			Subtotal -> (Total of this page)		$	
			Total -> (use only on last page of the completed Schedule E.)		$	

_____ Continuation sheets attached.

(Report total also on Summary of Schedules)

3072 © 1991 JULIUS BLUMBERG, INC., NYC 10013

SCHEDULE E (Continued)

Form B6 E Cont. (6-90)   Julius Blumberg, Inc. NYC 10013

In re: Debtor(s)   Case No.   (if known)

SCHEDULE E - CREDITORS HOLDING UNSECURED PRIORITY CLAIMS
(Continuation Sheet)

CREDITOR'S NAME AND MAILING ADDRESS INCLUDING ZIP CODE	CO DEBT	H W J C	DATE CLAIM WAS INCURRED AND CONSIDERATION FOR CLAIM	C U D	TOTAL AMOUNT OF CLAIM	AMOUNT ENTITLED TO PRIORITY
A/C #						
A/C #						
A/C #						
A/C #						
A/C #						
A/C #						
A/C #						
A/C #						
A/C #						

Sheet no. _____ of _____ sheets attached to Schedule of Creditors Holding Priority Claims.

Subtotal -> $ _____
(Total of this page)

Total -> $ _____
(use only on last page of completed Schedule E.)

(Report total also on Summary of Schedules)

3072 © 1991 JULIUS BLUMBERG, INC., NYC 10013

SCHEDULE E (Continued)

Form B6 E Cont. (6-90)   Julius Blumberg, Inc. NYC 10013

In re: Debtor(s)   Case No.   (if known)

SCHEDULE E - CREDITORS HOLDING UNSECURED PRIORITY CLAIMS
(Continuation Sheet)

CREDITOR'S NAME AND MAILING ADDRESS INCLUDING ZIP CODE	CODEBTOR	H W J C	DATE CLAIM WAS INCURRED AND CONSIDERATION FOR CLAIM	C U D	TOTAL AMOUNT OF CLAIM	AMOUNT ENTITLED TO PRIORITY
A/C #						
A/C #						
A/C #						
A/C #						
A/C #						
A/C #						
A/C #						
A/C #						
A/C #						

Sheet no. _____ of _____ sheets attached to Schedule of Creditors Holding Priority Claims.

Subtotal -> $
(Total of this page)

Total -> $
(use only on last page of completed Schedule E.)

(Report total also on Summary of Schedules)

3072 © 1991 JULIUS BLUMBERG, INC., NYC 10013

SCHEDULE E (Continued)

Form B6 E Cont. (6-90)　　　Julius Blumberg, Inc. NYC 10013

In re:

Debtor(s)　　Case No.　　　(if known)

SCHEDULE E - CREDITORS HOLDING UNSECURED PRIORITY CLAIMS
(Continuation Sheet)

CREDITOR'S NAME AND MAILING ADDRESS INCLUDING ZIP CODE	CO DEBT	H W J C	DATE CLAIM WAS INCURRED AND CONSIDERATION FOR CLAIM	C U D	TOTAL AMOUNT OF CLAIM	AMOUNT ENTITLED TO PRIORITY
A/C #						
A/C #						
A/C #						
A/C #						
A/C #						
A/C #						
A/C #						
A/C #						
A/C #						

Sheet no. _____ of _____ sheets attached to Schedule of Creditors Holding Priority Claims.

Subtotal -> $
(Total of this page)

Total -> $
(use only on last page of completed Schedule E.)

(Report total also on Summary of Schedules)

3072 © 1991 JULIUS BLUMBERG, INC., NYC 10013

SCHEDULE F

Julius Blumberg, Inc. NYC 10013

Blumbergs Law Products Form B6 F (6-90)

In re: _____ Debtor(s)   Case No. _____ (if known)

SCHEDULE F - CREDITORS HOLDING UNSECURED NONPRIORITY CLAIMS

☐ Check this box if debtor has no creditors holding unsecured nonpriority claims to report on this Schedule F

CREDITOR'S NAME AND MAILING ADDRESS INCLUDING ZIP CODE	CO DEBT	H W J C	DATE CLAIM WAS INCURRED AND CONSIDERATION FOR CLAIM. IF CLAIM IS SUBJECT TO SETOFF, SO STATE.	C U D	AMOUNT OF CLAIM
A/C #					
A/C #					
A/C #					
A/C #					
A/C #					
A/C #					
A/C #					
A/C #					
A/C #					

_____ Continuation Sheets attached.

Subtotal -> $ _____
(Total of this page)

Total -> $ _____
(use only on last page of completed Schedule F.)
(Report total also on Summary of Schedules)

3072 © 1991 JULIUS BLUMBERG, INC., NYC 10013

SCHEDULE F (Continued)

Form B6 F, Cont. (10-89)   Julius Blumberg, Inc. NYC 10013

In re: _____   Debtor(s)   Case No. _____   (if known)

SCHEDULE F - CREDITORS HOLDING UNSECURED NONPRIORITY CLAIMS
(Continuation Sheet)

CREDITOR'S NAME AND MAILING ADDRESS INCLUDING ZIP CODE	CODEBTOR	H W J C	DATE CLAIM WAS INCURRED AND CONSIDERATION FOR CLAIM. IF CLAIM IS SUBJECT TO SETOFF, SO STATE.	C U D	AMOUNT OF CLAIM
A/C #					
A/C #					
A/C #					
A/C #					
A/C #					
A/C #					
A/C #					
A/C #					
A/C #					

Sheet no. _____ of _____ sheets attached to Schedule of Creditors Holding Nonpriority Claims.

Subtotal -> $ _____
(Total of this page)

Total -> $ _____
(use only on last page of completed Schedule F.)
(Report total also on Summary of Schedules)

3072 © 1991 JULIUS BLUMBERG, INC., NYC 10013

SCHEDULE F (Continued)

Form B6 F, Cont. (10-89)   Julius Blumberg, Inc. NYC 10013

In re: Debtor(s)   Case No.   (if known)

SCHEDULE F - CREDITORS HOLDING UNSECURED NONPRIORITY CLAIMS
(Continuation Sheet)

CREDITOR'S NAME AND MAILING ADDRESS INCLUDING ZIP CODE	CO DEBT OR	H W J C	DATE CLAIM WAS INCURRED AND CONSIDERATION FOR CLAIM. IF CLAIM IS SUBJECT TO SETOFF, SO STATE.	C U D	AMOUNT OF CLAIM
A/C #					
A/C #					
A/C #					
A/C #					
A/C #					
A/C #					
A/C #					
A/C #					
A/C #					

Sheet no. _____ of _____ sheets attached to Schedule of Creditors Holding Nonpriority Claims.

Subtotal -> $
(Total of this page)

Total -> $
(use only on last page of completed Schedule F.)
(Report total also on Summary of Schedules)

SCHEDULE F (Continued)

Form B6 F, Cont. (10-89)   Julius Blumberg, Inc. NYC 10013

In re: Debtor(s)   Case No.   · (if known)

SCHEDULE F - CREDITORS HOLDING UNSECURED NONPRIORITY CLAIMS
(Continuation Sheet)

CREDITOR'S NAME AND MAILING ADDRESS INCLUDING ZIP CODE	CO DEBT	H W J C	DATE CLAIM WAS INCURRED AND CONSIDERATION FOR CLAIM. IF CLAIM IS SUBJECT TO SETOFF, SO STATE.	C U D	AMOUNT OF CLAIM
A/C #					
A/C #					
A/C #					
A/C #					
A/C #					
A/C #					
A/C #					
A/C #					
A/C #					

Sheet no. _____ of _____ sheets attached to Schedule of Creditors Holding Nonpriority Claims.

Subtotal -> $
(Total of this page)

Total -> $
(use only on last page of completed Schedule F.)
(Report total also on Summary of Schedules)

3072 © 1991 JULIUS BLUMBERG, INC., NYC 10013

SCHEDULE F (Continued)

Form B6 F, Cont. (10-89)   Julius Blumberg, Inc. NYC 10013

In re: Debtor(s)   Case No.   (if known)

SCHEDULE F - CREDITORS HOLDING UNSECURED NONPRIORITY CLAIMS
(Continuation Sheet)

CREDITOR'S NAME AND MAILING ADDRESS INCLUDING ZIP CODE	CO DEBT	H W J C	DATE CLAIM WAS INCURRED AND CONSIDERATION FOR CLAIM. IF CLAIM IS SUBJECT TO SETOFF, SO STATE.	C U D	AMOUNT OF CLAIM
A/C #					
A/C #					
A/C #					
A/C #					
A/C #					
A/C #					
A/C #					
A/C #					
A/C #					

Sheet no. _____ of _____ sheets attached to Schedule of Creditors Holding Nonpriority Claims.

Subtotal -> $
(Total of this page)

Total -> $
(use only on last page of completed Schedule F.)
(Report total also on Summary of Schedules)

3072 © 1991 JULIUS BLUMBERG, INC., NYC 10013

SCHEDULE G

Form B6 G (6-90)   Julius Blumberg, Inc. NYC 10013

In re: Debtor(s)   Case No.   (if known)

SCHEDULE G - EXECUTORY CONTRACTS AND UNEXPIRED LEASES

☐ Check this box if debtor has no executory contracts or unexpired leases.

NAME AND MAILING ADDRESS, INCLUDING ZIP CODE, OF OTHER PARTIES TO LEASE OR CONTRACT.	DESCRIPTION OF CONTRACT OR LEASE AND NATURE OF DEBTOR'S INTEREST. STATE WHETHER LEASE IS FOR NONRESIDENTIAL REAL PROPERTY. STATE CONTRACT NUMBER OF ANY GOVERNMENT CONTRACT.

Forms may be purchased from Julius Blumberg, Inc., NYC 10013, or any of its dealers. Reproduction prohibited.

SCHEDULE H

Form B6 H, (6-90)   Julius Blumberg, Inc. NYC 10013

In re: Debtor(s)   Case No.   (If known)

SCHEDULE H - CODEBTORS

☐ Check this box if debtor has no codebtors.

NAME AND ADDRESS OF CODEBTOR	NAME AND ADDRESS OF CREDITOR

SAMPLE

3072 © 1991 JULIUS BLUMBERG, INC., NYC 10013

SCHEDULE I

Form B6I (6-90)   Julius Blumberg, Inc. NYC 10013

In re: Debtor(s)   Case No.   (if known)

SCHEDULE I - CURRENT INCOME OF INDIVIDUAL DEBTOR(S)

The column labeled "Spouse" must be completed in all cases filed by joint debtors and by a married debtor in a chapter 12 or 13 case whether or not a joint petition is filed, unless the spouses are separated and a joint petition is not filed.

Debtor's Marital Status:	DEPENDENTS OF DEBTOR AND SPOUSE		
	NAMES	AGE	RELATIONSHIP

Employment:	DEBTOR	SPOUSE
Occupation		
Name of Employer		
How long employed		
Address of Employer		

Income: (Estimate of average monthly income)   DEBTOR   SPOUSE

Current monthly gross wages, salary, and commissions (pro rate if not paid monthly.) .... $ _____ $ _____

Estimate monthly overtime .... _____ _____

SUBTOTAL .... $ _____ $ _____

     LESS PAYROLL DEDUCTIONS

      a. Payroll taxes and social security .... _____ _____

      b. Insurance .... _____ _____

      c. Union dues .... _____ _____

      d. Other (Specify) ....

SUBTOTAL OF PAYROLL DEDUCTIONS .... $ _____ $ _____

TOTAL NET MONTHLY TAKE HOME PAY .... $ _____ $ _____

Regular income from operation of business or profession or farm

(attach detailed statement) ....

Income from real property ....

Interest and dividends ....

Alimony, maintenance or support payments payable to the debtor for the debtor's

   use or that of dependents listed above.

Social security or other government assistance (Specify) .....

Pension or retirement income ....

Other monthly income (Specify) ....

TOTAL MONTHLY INCOME .... $ _____ $ _____

TOTAL COMBINED MONTHLY INCOME $ _____   (Report also on Summary of Schedules)

Describe any increase or decrease of more than 10% in any of the above categories anticipated to occur within the year following the filing of this document:

3072 © 1991 JULIUS BLUMBERG, INC., NYC 10013

SCHEDULE I (Continued)

Form B6I & J (6-90)   Julius Blumberg, Inc., NYC 10013

Blumberg
Law Products

In re   Debtor   Case No.   (if known)

SCHEDULE I - CURRENT INCOME OF DEBTOR

SAMPLE

Total $

SCHEDULE J

SCHEDULE J - CURRENT EXPENDITURES OF DEBTOR

Total $

Note: Estimate monthly income and expenditures.

5024/J © 1991 JULIUS BLUMBERG. INC.. NYC 10013

SAMPLE

Forms may be purchased from Julius Blumberg, Inc., NYC 10013, or any of its dealers. Reproduction prohibited.

SCHEDULE J (Continued)

Form B6 J, Cont. (6-90)   Julius Blumberg, Inc. NYC 10013

In re: Debtor(s)   Case No.   · (if known)

SCHEDULE J - CURRENT EXPENDITURES OF INDIVIDUAL DEBTOR(S)

Complete this schedule by estimating the average monthly expenses of the debtor and the debtor's family. Pro rate any payments made bi-weekly, quarterly, semi-annually, or annually to show monthly rate.

☐ Check this box if a joint petition is filed and debtor's spouse maintains a separate household. Complete a separate schedule of expenditures labeled "Spouse".

Rent or home mortgage payment (include lot rented for mobile home) .... $

Are real estate taxes included?   ☐ Yes   ☐ No   Is property insurance included?   ☐ Yes   ☐ No

Utilities Electricity and heating fuel ....

Water and sewer ....

Telephone ....

Other

Home maintenance (repairs and upkeep) ....

Food ....

Clothing ....

Laundry and dry cleaning ....

Medical and dental expenses ....

Transportation (not including car payments) ....

Recreation, clubs and entertainment, newspapers, magazines, etc. ....

Charitable contributions ....

Insurance (not deducted from wages or included in home mortgage payments)

Homeowner's or renter's ....

Life ....

Health ....

Auto ....

Other

Taxes (not deducted from wages or included in home mortgage payments)

(Specify)

Installment payments: (In chapter 12 and 13 cases, do not list payments to be included in the plan)

Auto ....

Other

Alimony, maintenance, and support paid to others ....

Payments for support of additional dependents not living at your home ....

Regular expenses from operation of business, profession, or farm (attach detailed statement) ....

Other

TOTAL MONTHLY EXPENSES (Report also on Summary of Schedules) .... $ _____

(FOR CHAPTER 12 AND 13 DEBTORS ONLY)
Provide the information requested below, including whether plan payments are to be made bi-weekly, monthly, annually, or at some other regular interval.

A. Total projected monthly income .... $

B. Total projected monthly expenses .... $ _____

C. Excess income (A minus B) .... $ _____

D. Total amount to be paid into plan each .... $ _____
                                    (interval)

3072 © 1991 JULIUS BLUMBERG, INC., NYC 10013

DECLARATION CONCERNING DEBTOR'S SCHEDULES

Form B6 Cont. (6-90)   Julius Blumberg, Inc. N Y C 10013

In re:

                                                        Debtor(s)   Case No.

                                                                                              (if known)

DECLARATION CONCERNING DEBTOR'S SCHEDULES

DECLARATION UNDER PENALTY OF PERJURY BY INDIVIDUAL DEBTOR

I declare under penalty of perjury that I have read the foregoing summary and schedules, consisting of _____ sheets, and that

they are true and correct to the best of my knowledge, information, and belief.   (Total shown on summary page plus 1.)

Date   Signature: _____
                                                                          Debtor

Date   Signature: _____
                                                                   (Joint Debtor, if any)
                                                        (If joint case, both spouses must sign.)

DECLARATION UNDER PENALTY OF PERJURY ON BEHALF OF CORPORATION OR PARTNERSHIP

I, the _____ (the president or other officer or an authorized agent of the corporation or a member or an

authorized agent of the partnership) of the _____ (corporation or partnership) named as debtor in this case,

declare under penalty of perjury that I have read the foregoing summary and schedules, consisting of _____ sheets, and

that they are true and correct to the best of my knowledge, information, and belief.   (Total shown on summary page plus 1.)

Date   Signature: _____

                                                        (Pint or type name of individual signing on behalf of debtor.)

                              (An individual signing on behalf of a partnership or corporation must indicate position or relationship to debtor.)

Penalty for making a false statement or concealing property: Fine of up to $500,000 or imprisonment for up to 5 years or both. 18 U.S.C. §§ 152 and 3571.

DECLARATION CONCERNING DEBTOR'S SCHEDULES (Continued)

UNITED STATES BANKRUPTCY COURT

_____DISTRICT OF_____

<table>
<tr><td></td><td>Chapter_____</td><td rowspan="2">FOR COURT USE ONLY
Date Petition Filed _____
Bankruptcy Judge _____</td></tr>
<tr><td>In re_____</td><td>Case No. _____</td></tr>
<tr><td>Debtor</td><td></td></tr>
</table>

REAFFIRMATION AGREEMENT

The undersigned Debtor(s) reaffirms the following debt on the terms set forth.

(1) Name of creditor (including last known holder of any negotiable instrument) and complete mailing address including zip code.	(2) Specify when claim was incurred and the consideration therefor; when claim is contingent, unliquidated, disputed, subject to setoff, evidenced by a judgment, negotiable instrument, or other writing, or incurred as partner or joint contractor, so indicate; specify name of any partner or joint contractor on any debt.	(3) Indicate if claim is contingent, unliquidated, or disputed.	(4) H W or J	(5) Amount of Claim
				$

☐ The terms of the reaffirmation are as follows:

SAMPLE

☐ The terms of the reaffirmation are set forth on the Creditor's form of Reaffirmation Agreement annexed.

_____   _____   _____   _____
Date   Signature of Creditor   Date   Signature of Debtor

_____
Signature of Debtor

NOTICE TO DEBTOR

This agreement may be rescinded at any time prior to discharge or within 60 days after this agreement is filed with the court, whichever occurs later, by giving notice of rescission to the holder of this claim.

DECLARATION OF ATTORNEY

I, _____ the attorney that represented the Debtor(s) during the negotiation of the above agreement, declare that this agreement (a) represents a fully informed and voluntary agreement by the Debtor(s), and (b) does not impose an undue hardship on the Debtor(s) or a dependent of the Debtor(s).

Executed on _____   _____
                                                                    Signature of Attorney for Debtor(s)

CHAPTER 7 STATEMENT OF INTENTION

Form B8 (6-90)   Julius Blumberg, Inc. NYC 10013

UNITED STATES BANKRUPTCY COURT   **DISTRICT OF**

In re: Debtor(s)   Case No.
                                                               Chapter

CHAPTER 7 INDIVIDUAL DEBTOR'S STATEMENT OF INTENTION

1. I, the debtor, have filed a schedule of assets and liabilities which includes consumer debts secured by property of the estate.

2. My intention with respect to the property of the estate which secures those consumer debts is as follows:

   a. *Property to Be Surrendered.*

Description of property	Creditor's name	H,W or J

   b. *Property to Be Retained (Specify Reaff'd, Red'd or Exempt to state debtor's intention concerning reaffirmation, redemption, or lien avoidance).*

Description of property	Creditor's name	Reaff'd Red'd Exempt

3. I understand that § 521(2)(B) of the Bankruptcy Code requires that I perform the above stated intention within 45 days of the filing of this statement with the court, or within such additional time as the court, for cause, within such 45-day period fixes.

Date:

....
Signature of Debtor

* **Reaff'd** - Debt will be reaffirmed pursuant to § 524(c)

  Red'd - Property is claimed as exempt and will be redeemed pursuant to § 722

  Exempt - Lien will be avoided pursuant to § 522(f) and property will be claimed as exempt

....
Signature of Debtor

LIST OF UNSECURED CREDITORS

Form B4 (6-90)   Julius Blumberg, Inc. NYC 10013

UNITED STATES BANKRUPTCY COURT   **DISTRICT OF**

In re: Debtor(s)   Case No.   (If Known)

LIST OF CREDITORS HOLDING 20 LARGEST UNSECURED CLAIMS

Following is the list of the debtor's creditors holding the 20 largest unsecured claims. The list is prepared in accordance with Fed. R. Bankr. P. 1007(d) for filing in this chapter 11 [or chapter 9] case. The list does not include (1) persons who come within the definition of "insider" set forth in 11 U.S.C. § 101(30), or (2) secured creditors unless the value of the collateral is such that the unsecured deficiency places the creditor among the holders of the 20 largest unsecured claims

(1) NAME OF CREDITOR AND COMPLETE MAILING ADDRESS INCLUDING ZIP CODE	(2) NAME, TELEPHONE NUMBER AND COMPLETE MAILING ADDRESS, INCLUDING ZIP CODE OF EMPLOYEE, AGENT, OR DEPARTMENT OF CREDITOR FAMILIAR WITH CLAIM.	(3) NATURE OF CLAIM (trade debt, bank loan, government contract, etc)	(4) C U D S	(5) AMOUNT OF CLAIM (If secured also state value of security)

"(4) C U D S" If contingent, enter C; if unliquidated, enter U; if disputed, enter D; if subject to setoff, enter S.

3085-1 © 1991 JULIUS BLUMBERG, INC., NYC 10013

LIST OF UNSECURED CREDITORS (Continued)

Form B4 (6-90)   Julius Blumberg, Inc. NYC 10013

LIST OF CREDITORS HOLDING 20 LARGEST UNSECURED CLAIMS (continuation)

(1)	(2)	(3)	(4)	(5)

Unsworn Declaration under Penalty of Perjury (partnership or corporation) I declare under penalty of perjury that I have read the answers contained in the foregoing list of creditors and that they are true and corrrect to the best of my knowledge, information and belief.

_____ _____ _____
Date   **Signature**   **Print Name and Title**

(An individual signing on behalf of a partnership or corporation must indicate position or relationship to debtor.)

Penalty for making a false statement: Fine of up to $500.00 or imprisonment for up to 5 years, or both. 18 U.S.C. § § 152 and 3571

3085-2 © 1991 JULIUS BLUMBERG, INC., NYC 10013

Forms may be purchased from Julius Blumberg, Inc., NYC 10013, or any of its dealers. Reproduction prohibited.

LIST OF EQUITY SECURITY HOLDERS

3087   Equity security holders list, chapter 11, 8-91

UNITED STATES BANKRUPTCY COURT   **DISTRICT OF**

In re   Debtor(s)   Case No.   (If Known)

LIST OF EQUITY SECURITY HOLDERS

Registered name of holder of security Last know address or place business	Class of security	Number registered	Kind of interest registered

STATEMENT OF FINANCIAL AFFAIRS

 Form 7 Stmt. of Financial
Affairs (8-91)

Julius Blumberg, Inc.
NYC 10013

UNITED STATES BANKRUPTCY COURT

DISTRICT OF

In re:

Debtor(s)   *Case No.*

STATEMENT OF FINANCIAL AFFAIRS

This statement is to be completed by every debtor. Spouses filing a joint petition may file a single statement on which the information for both spouses is combined. If the case is filed under chapter 12 or chapter 13, a married debtor must furnish information for both spouses whether or not a joint petition is filed, unless the spouses are separated and a joint petition is not filed. An individual debtor engaged in business as a sole proprietor, partner, family farmer, or self-employed professional, should provide the information requested on this statement concerning all such activities as well as the invididual's personal affairs.

Questions 1-15 are to be completed by all debtors. Debtors that are or have been in business, as defined below, also must complete Questions 16-21. **Each question must be answered. If the answer to any question is "None," or the question is not applicable, mark the box labeled "None."** If additional space is needed for the answer to any question, use and attach a separate sheet properly identified with the case name, case number (if known), and the number of the question.

DEFINITIONS

"In business." A debtor is "in business" for the purpose of this form if the debtor is a corporation or partnership. An individual debtor is "in business" for the purpose of this form if the debtor is or has been, within the two years immediately preceding the filing of this bankruptcy case, any of the following: an officer, director, managing executive, or person in control of a corporation; a partner, other than a limited partner, of a partnership; a sole proprietor or self-employed.

"Insider." The term "insider" includes but is not limited to: relatives of the debtor; general partners of the debtor and their relatives; corporations of which the debtor is an officer, director, or person in control; officers, directors, and any person in control of a corporate debtor and their relatives; affiliates of the debtor and insiders of such affiliates; any managing agent of the debtor. 11 U.S.C. §101(30).

☐ None   **1. Income from Employment or Operation of Business**

State the gross amount of income the debtor has received from employment, trade, or profession, or from operation of the debtor's business from the beginning of this calendar year to the date this case was commenced. State also the gross amounts received during the **two years** immediately preceding this calendar year. (A debtor that maintains, or has maintained, financial records on the basis of a fiscal rather than a calendar year may report fiscal year income. Identify the beginning and ending dates of the debtor's fiscal year.) If a joint petition is filed, state income for each spouse separately. (Married debtors filing under chapter 12 or chapter 13 must state income of both spouses whether or not a joint petition is filed, unless the spouses are separated and a joint petition is not filed.)

Give AMOUNT and SOURCE (If more than one).

☐ None   **2. Income Other than from Employment or Operation of Business**

State the amount of income received by the debtor other than from employment, trade, profession, or operation of the debtor's business during the two years immediately preceding the commencement of this case. Give particulars. If a joint petition is filed, state income for each spouse separately. (Married debtors filing under chapter 12 or chapter 13 must state income for each spouse whether or not a joint petition is filed, unless the spouses are separated and a joint petition is not filed.)

Give AMOUNT and SOURCE.

3. Payments to Creditors

☐ None   a. List all payments on loans, installment purchases of goods or services, and other debts, aggregating more than $600 to any creditor, made within **90 days** immediately preceding the commencement of this case. (Married debtors filing under chapter 12 or chapter 13 must include payments by either or both spouses whether or not a joint petition is filed, unless the spouses are separated and a joint petition is not filed.)

Give NAME AND ADDRESS OF CREDITOR, DATES OF PAYMENTS, AMOUNT PAID and AMOUNT STILL OWING.

☐ None   b. List all payments made within **one year** immediately preceding the commencement of this case to or for the benefit of creditors who are or were insiders. (Married debtors filing under chapter 12 or chapter 13 must include payments by either or both spouses whether or not a joint petition is filed, unless the spouses are separated and a joint petition is not filed.)

Give NAME AND ADDRESS OF CREDITOR AND RELATIONSHIP TO DEBTOR, DATE OF PAYMENT, AMOUNT PAID and AMOUNT STILL OWING.

4. Suits, Executions, Garnishments and Attachments

☐ None   a. List all suits to which the debtor is or was a party within **one year** immediately preceding the filing of this bankruptcy case. (Married debtors filing under chapter 12 or chapter 13 must include information concerning either or both spouses whether or not a joint petition is filed, unless the spouses are separated and a joint petition is not filed.)

Give CAPTION OF SUIT AND CASE NUMBER, NATURE OF PROCEEDING, COURT AND LOCATION and STATUS OR DISPOSTION.

☐ None   b. Describe all property that has been attached, garnished, or seized under any legal or equitable process within **one year**

STATEMENT OF FINANCIAL AFFAIRS (Continued)

immediately preceding the commencement of this case. (Married debtors filing under chapter 12 or chapter 13 must include information concerning property of either or both spouses whether or not a joint petition is filed, unless the spouses are separated and a joint petition is not filed.)

Give NAME AND ADDRESS OF PERSON FOR WHOSE BENEFIT PROPERTY WAS SEIZED, DATE OF SEIZURE and DESCRIPTION AND VALUE OF PROPERTY.

☐ None   **5. Repossessions, Foreclosures, and Returns**

List all property that has been repossessed by a creditor, sold at a foreclosure sale, transferred through a deed in lieu of foreclosure or returned to the seller, within **one year** immediately preceding the commencement of this case. (Married debtors filing under chapter 12 or chapter 13 must include information concerning property of either or both spouses whether or not a joint petition is filed, unless the spouses are separated and a joint petition is not filed.)

Give NAME AND ADDRESS OF CREDITOR OR SELLER, DATE OF REPOSSESSION, FORECLOSURE SALE, TRANSFER OR RETURN and DESCRIPTION AND VALUE OF PROPERTY.

6. Assignments and Receiverships

☐ None   a. Describe any assignment of property for the benefit of creditors made within **120 days** immediately preceding the commencement of this case. (Married debtors filing under chapter 12 or chapter 13 must include any assignment by either or both spouses whether or not a joint petition is filed, unless the spouses are separated and a joint petition is not filed.)

Give NAME AND ADDRESS OF ASSIGNEE, DATE OF ASSIGNMENT and TERMS OF ASSIGNMENT OR SETTLEMENT.

☐ None   b. List all property which has been in the hands of a custodian, receiver, or court-appointed official within **one year** immediately preceding the commencement of this case. (Married debtors filing under chapter 12 or chapter 13 must include information concerning property of either or both spouses whether or not a joint petition is filed, unless the spouses are separated and a joint petition is not filed.)

Give NAME AND ADDRESS OF CUSTODIAN, NAME AND LOCATION OF COURT, CASE TITLE & NUMBER, DATE OF ORDER and DESCRIPTION AND VALUE OF PROPERTY.

☐ None   **7. Gifts**

List all gifts or charitable contributions made within **one year** immediately preceding the commencement of this case except ordinary and usual gifts to family members aggregating less than $200 in value per individual family member and charitable contributions aggregating less than $100 per recipient. (Married debtors filing under chapter 12 or chapter 13 must include gifts or contributions by either or both spouses whether or not a joint petition is filed, unless the spouses are separated and a joint petition is not filed.)

Give NAME AND ADDRESS OF PERSON OR ORGANIZATION, RELATIONSHIP TO DEBTOR, IF ANY, DATE OF GIFT, and DESCRIPTION AND VALUE OF GIFT.

☐ None   **8. Losses**

List all losses from fire, theft, other casualty or gambling within **one year** immediately preceding the commencement of this case **or since the commencement of this case.** (Married debtors filing under chapter 12 or chapter 13 must include losses by either or both spouses whether or not a joint petition is filed, unless the spouses are separated and a joint petition is not filed.)

Give DESCRIPTION AND VALUE OF PROPERTY, DESCRIPTION OF CIRCUMSTANCES AND, IF LOSS WAS COVERED IN WHOLE OR IN PART BY INSURANCE, GIVE PARTICULARS and DATE OF LOSS.

☐ None   **9. Payments Related to Debt Counseling or Bankruptcy**

List all payments made or property transferred by or on behalf of the debtor to any persons, including attorneys, for consultation concerning debt consolidation, relief under the bankruptcy law or preparation of a petition in bankruptcy within **one year** immediately preceding the commencement of this case.

Give NAME AND ADDRESS OF PAYEE, DATE OF PAYMENT, NAME OF PAYOR IF OTHER THAN DEBTOR and AMOUNT OF MONEY OR DESCRIPTION AND VALUE OF PROPERTY.

☐ None   **10. Other Transfers**

List all other property, other than property transferred in the ordinary course of the business or financial affairs of the debtor, transferred either absolutely or as security within **one year** immediately preceding the commencement of this case. (Married debtors filing under chapter 12 or chapter 13 must include transfers by either or both spouses whether or not a joint petition is filed, unless the spouses are separated and a joint petition is not filed.)

Give NAME AND ADDRESS OF TRANSFEREE, RELATIONSHIP TO DEBTOR, DATE, and DESCRIBE PROPERTY TRANSFERRED AND VALUE RECEIVED.

STATEMENT OF FINANCIAL AFFAIRS (Continued)

☐ None   **11. Closed Financial Accounts**

List all financial accounts and instruments held in the name of the debtor or for the benefit of the debtor which were closed, sold, or otherwise transferred within **one year** immediately preceding the commencement of this case. Include checking, savings, or other financial accounts, certificates of deposit, or other instruments; shares and share accounts held in banks, credit unions, pension funds, cooperatives, associations, brokerage houses and other financial institutions. (Married debtors filing under chapter 12 or chapter 13 must include information concerning accounts or instruments held by or for either or both spouses whether or not a joint petition is filed, unless the spouses are separated and a joint petition is not filed.)

Give NAME AND ADDRESS OF INSTITUTION, TYPE AND NUMBER OF AC-COUNT AND AMOUNT OF FINAL BALANCE and AMOUNT AND DATE OF SALE OR CLOSING.

☐ None   **12. Safe Deposit Boxes**

List each safe deposit or other box or depository in which the debtor has or had securities, cash, or other valuables within **one year** immediately preceding the commencement of this case. (Married debtors filing under chapter 12 or chapter 13 must include boxes or depositories of either or both spouses whether or not a joint petition is filed, unless the spouses are separated and a joint petition is not filed.)

Give NAME AND ADDRESS OF BANK OR OTHER DEPOSITORY, NAMES AND ADDRESSES OF THOSE WITH ACCESS TO BOX OR DEPOSITORY, DESCRIPTION OF CONTENTS and DATE OF TRANSFER OR SURRENDER, IF ANY.

☐ None   **13. Setoffs**

List all setoffs made by any creditor, including a bank, against a debt or deposit of the debtor within **90 days** preceding the commencement of this case. (Married debtors filing under chapter 12 or chapter 13 must include information concerning either or both spouses whether or not a joint petition is filed, unless the spouses are separated and a joint petition is not filed.)

Give NAME AND ADDRESS OR CREDITOR, DATE OF SETOFF and AMOUNT OF SETOFF.

☐ None   **14. Property Held for Another Person**

List all property owned by another person that the debtor holds or controls.

Give NAME AND ADDRESS OF OWNER, DESCRIPTION AND VALUE OF PROPERTY and LOCATION OF PROPERTY.

☐ None   **15. Prior Address of Debtor**

If the debtor has moved within the two years immediately preceding the commencement of this case, list all premises which the debtor occupied during that period and vacated prior to the commencement of this case. If a joint petition is filed, report also any separate address of either spouse.

Give ADDRESS, NAME USED and DATES OF OCCUPANCY.

The following questions are to be completed as shown below.*

16. Nature, Location and Name of Business*

☐ None   a. If the debtor is an individual, list the names and addresses of all businesses in which the debtor was an officer, director, partner, or managing executive of a corporation, partnership, sole proprietorship or was a self-employed professional within the **two years** immediately preceding the commencement of this case, or in which the debtor owned 5 percent or more of the voting or equity securities within the two years immediately preceding the commencement of this case.

b. If the debtor is a partnership, list the names and addresses of all businesses in which the debtor was a partner or owned 5 percent or more of the voting securities, within the **two years** immediately preceding the commencement of this case.

c. If the debtor is a corporation, list the names and addresses of all businesses in which the debtor was a partner or owned 5 percent or more of the voting securities within the **two years** immediately preceding the commencement of this case.

Give NAME, ADDRESS, NATURE OF BUSINESS and BEGINNING AND ENDING DATES OF OPERATION.

17. Books, Records, and Financial Statements

☐ None   a. List all bookkeepers and accountants who within the **six years** immediately preceding the filing of this bankruptcy case kept or supervised the keeping of books of account and records of the debtor.

Give NAME AND ADDRESS and DATES SERVICES RENDERED.

*These questions are to be completed by every debtor that is a corporation or partnership and by any individual debtor who is or has been, within the two years immediately preceding the commencement of this case, any of the following: an officer, director, managing executive, or owner of more than 5 percent of the voting securities of a corporation; a partner, other than a limited partner, of a partnership; a sole proprietor or otherwise self-employed. (An individual or joint debtor should complete this portion of the statement only if the debtor is or has been in business, as defined above, within the two years immediately preceding the commencement of this case.)

STATEMENT OF FINANCIAL AFFAIRS (Continued)

☐ None   b. List all firms or individuals who within the **two years** immediately preceding the filing of this bankruptcy case have audited the books of account and records, or prepared a financial statement of the debtor.
Give NAME, ADDRESS and DATES SERVICES RENDERED.

☐ None   c. List all firms or individuals who at the time of the commencement of this case were in possession of the books of account and records of the debtor. If any of the books of account and records are not available, explain.
Give NAME and ADDRESS.

☐ None   d. List all financial institutions, creditors and other parties, including mercantile and trade agencies, to whom a financial statement was issued within the **two years** immediately preceding the commencement of this case by the debtor.
Give NAME AND ADDRESS and DATE ISSUED.

18. Inventories

☐ None   a. List the dates of the last two inventories taken of your property, the name of the person who supervised the taking of each inventory, and the dollar amount and basis of each inventory.
Give DATE OF INVENTORY, INVENTORY, SUPERVISOR and DOLLAR AMOUNT OF INVENTORY (specify cost, market or other basis).

☐ None   b. List the name and address of the person having possession of the records of each of the two inventories reported in a., above.
Give DATE OF INVENTORY and NAME AND ADDRESSES OF CUSTODIAN OF INVENTORY RECORDS.

19. Current Partners, Officers, Directors and Shareholders

☐ None   a. If the debtor is a partnership, list the nature and percentage of partnership interest of each member of the partnership.
Give NAME AND ADDRESS, NATURE OF INTEREST and PERCENTAGE OF INTEREST.

☐ None   b. If the debtor is a corporation, list all officers and directors of the corporation, and each stockholder who directly or indirectly owns, controls, or holds 5 percent or more of the voting securities of the corporation.
Give NAME AND ADDRESS, TITLE and NATURE AND PERCENTAGE OF STOCK OWNERSHIP.

20. Former Partners, Officers, Directors and Shareholders

☐ None   a. If the debtor is a partnership, list each member who withdrew from the partnership within **one year** immediately preceding the commencement of this case.
Give NAME, ADDRESS and DATE OF WITHDRAWAL.

☐ None   b. If the debtor is a corporation, list all officers or directors whose relationship with the corporation terminated within **one year** immediately preceding the commencement of this case.
Give NAME AND ADDRESS, TITLE and DATE OF TERMINATION.

☐ None   **21. Withdrawals from a Partnership or Distributions by a Corporation**

If the debtor is a partnership or corporation, list all withdrawals or distributions credited or given to an insider, including compensation in any form, bonuses, loans, stock redemptions, options exercised and any other perquisite during **one year** immediately preceding the commencement of this case.
Give NAME & ADDRESS OF RECIPIENT, RELATIONSHIP TO DEBTOR, DATE AND PURPOSE OF WITHDRAWAL, and AMOUNT OF MONEY OR DESCRIPTION AND VALUE OF PROPERTY.

Unsworn Declaration under Penalty of Perjury.

(If completed by an individual or individual and spouse)   I declare under penalty of perjury that I have read the answers contained in the foregoing statement of financial affairs and any attachments thereto and that they are true and correct.

_____   _____   _____   _____
        Date   Signature of Debtor   Date   Signature of Joint Debtor (if any)

(If completed on behalf of a partnership or corporation)   I declare under penalty of perjury that I have read the answers contained in the foregoing statement of financial affairs and any attachments thereto and that they are true and correct to the best of my knowledge, information and belief.

_____   _____   _____
        Date   Signature   Print Name and Title

(An individual signing on behalf of a partnership or corporation must indicate position or relationship to debtor.)   _____ continuation sheets attached

Penalty for making a false statement: Fine of up to $500,000 or imprisonment for up to 5 years, or both. 18 U.S.C. §§152 and 3571.

ORDER AND NOTICE FOR HEARING ON DISCLOSURE STATEMENT

UNITED STATES BANKRUPTCY COURT

_____ **DISTRICT OF** _____

In re _____)
    [Set forth here all names including)
    married, maiden, and trade names used)
    by debtor within last 6 years])
)
              Debtor)   Case No. _____
)
)   Chapter _____
Social Security No(s). _____ and all)
Employer's Tax Identification No(s). [if any])
_____)

ORDER AND NOTICE FOR HEARING
ON DISCLOSURE STATEMENT

To the debtor, its creditors, and other parties in20interest:

    A disclosure statement and a plan under Chapter 11 of the Bankruptcy Code having been filed by _____ on _____, IT IS ORDERED and notice is hereby given, that:

    1.   The hearing to consider the approval of the disclosure statement shall be held at: _____, on _____, at _____ o'clock ____m.

    2.   _____ is fixed as the last day for filing and serving in accordance with Fed. R. Bankr. P. 3017(a) written objections to the disclosure statement.

    3.   Within _____ days after entry of this order, the disclosure statement and plan shall be distributed in accordance with Fed. R. Bankr. P. 3017(a).

    4.   Requests for copies of the disclosure statement and plan shall be mailed to the debtor in possession [or trustee or debtor or _____] at _____ (state mailing address) _____.

Dated: _____

                          BY THE COURT

                       _____
                       United States Bankruptcy Judge

ORDER CONFIRMING PLAN

UNITED STATES BANKRUPTCY COURT

_____ DISTRICT OF _____

In re _____   )
    [Set forth here all names including   )
    married, maiden, and trade names used   )
    by debtor within last 6 years]   )
)
) Case No. _____
                Debtor   )
) Chapter _____
Social Security No(s). _____ and all   )
Employer's Tax Identification No(s). [if any])
    _____   )

ORDER CONFIRMING PLAN

    The plan under Chapter 11 of the Bankruptcy Code filed by _____
on _____ [_if applicable,_ as modified by a modification filed on
_____,] or a summary thereof, having been transmitted to creditors and
equity security holders; and

    It having been determined after hearing on notice that the requirements for
confirmation set forth in 11 U.S.C. § 1129(a) [or, _if appropriate,_ 11 U.S.C. § 1129(b)]
have been satisfied;

    IT IS ORDERED that:

    The plan filed by _____, on _____,
[_If appropriate, include dates and any other pertinent details of modifications of the plan_]
is confirmed. A copy of the confirmed plan is attached.

Dated: _____

                                 BY THE COURT

                                _____
                                United States Bankruptcy Judge

CHAPTER 13 PLAN

3082   Chapter 13 Plan, 8-91

Blumbergs
Law Products

UNITED STATES BANKRUPTCY COURT   **DISTRICT OF**

In re   Debtor(s)   Case No.   (If Known)

CHAPTER 13 PLAN

(If this form is used by joint debtors wherever the word "debtor" or words referring to debtor are used they shall be read as if in the plural.)

1. The future earnings of the debtor are submitted to the supervision and control of the trustee and the *debtor — debtor's employer* shall pay to the trustee the sum of $ *weekly — bi-weekly — semi-monthly — monthly*   for a period of

2. From the payments so received, the trustee shall make disbursements as follows:
   (a) Full payment in deferred cash payments of all claims entitled to priority under 11 U.S.C. §507.

   (b) Holders of allowed secured claims shall retain the liens securing such claims and shall be paid as follows:

   (c) Subsequent to — pro rata with dividends to secured creditors, dividends to unsecured creditors whose claims are duly allowed as follows:

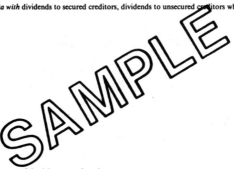

3. The following executory contracts of the debtor are rejected:

Title to the debtor's property shall revest in the debtor *on confirmation of a plan — upon dismissal of the case after confirmation pursuant to 11 U.S.C. §350.*

Dated: ....
                                        Debtor   *Debtor*

Acceptances may be mailed to..   ....
                                                                        Post Office Address

PROOF OF CLAIM

T 1031—Proof of claim, Official Form 10, power of attorney, Official Form 11A, 8-91.

Blumbergs Law Products

JULIUS BLUMBERG, INC.
PUBLISHER, NYC 10013

FORM B10 (6-90)

FORM 10. PROOF OF CLAIM

United States Bankruptcy Court	PROOF OF CLAIM
_____ District of _____	
In re (Name of Debtor)	Case Number

NOTE: This form should not be used to make a claim for an administrative expense arising after the commencement of the case. A "request" of payment of an administrative expense may be filed pursuant to 11 U.S.C. §503.

Name of Creditor *(The person or entity to whom the debtor owes money or property)*	☐ Check box if you are aware that anyone else has filed a proof of claim relating to your claim. Attach copy of statement giving particulars.
Name and Addresses Where Notices Should be Sent	☐ Check box if you have never received any notices from the bankruptcy court in this case.
	☐ Check box if the address differs from the address on the envelope sent to you by the court.
Telephone No.	THIS SPACE IS FOR COURT USE ONLY

ACCOUNT OR OTHER NUMBER BY WHICH CREDITOR IDENTIFIES DEBTOR:

Check here if this claim ☐ replaces ☐ amends a previously filed claim, dated _____

1. BASIS FOR CLAIM
- ☐ Goods sold
- ☐ Services performed
- ☐ Money loaned
- ☐ Personal injury/wrongful death
- ☐ Taxes
- ☐ Other (Describe briefly) _____

- ☐ Retiree benefits as defined in 11 U.S.C. §1114(a)
- ☐ Wages, salaries, and compensations (Fill out below)
  Your social security number _____
  Unpaid compensations for services performed from (date) _____ to _____ (date)

2. DATE DEBT WAS INCURRED

3. IF COURT JUDGMENT, DATE OBTAINED

4. CLASSIFICATION OF CLAIM. Under the Bankruptcy Code all claims are classified as one or more of the following: (1) Unsecured Nonpriority, (2) Unsecured Priority, (3) Secured. It is possible for part of a claim to be in one category and part in another. CHECK THE APPROPRIATE BOX OR BOXES that best describe your claim and STATE THE AMOUNT OF THE CLAIM.

☐ SECURED CLAIM $_____
Attach evidence of perfection of security interest.
Brief Description of Collateral:
- ☐ Real Estate ☐ Motor Vehicle ☐ Other (Describe briefly)

Amount of arrearage and other charges included in secured claim above, if any $_____

☐ UNSECURED NONPRIORITY CLAIM $_____
A claim is unsecured if there is no collateral or lien on prpoerty of the debtor securing the claim or to the extent that the value of such property is less than the amount of the claim.

☐ UNSECURED PRIORITY CLAIM $_____
Specify the priority of the claim.
- ☐ Wages, salaries, or commissions (up to $2000), earned not more than 90 days before filing of the bankruptcy petition or cessation of the debtor's business, whichever is earlier - 11 U.S.C. §507(a)(3)
- ☐ Contributions to an employee benefit plan - 11 U.S.C. §507(a)(4)
- ☐ Up to $900 of deposits toward purchase, lease, or rental of property or services for personal, family, or household use - 11 U.S.C. §507(a)(6)
- ☐ Taxes or penalties of governmental units - 11 U.S.C. §507(a)(7)
- ☐ Other - 11 U.S.C. §§507 (a)(2), (a)(5) - (Describe briefly)

5. TOTAL AMOUNT OF CLAIM AT TIME CASE FILED:
$_____ (Unsecured) $_____ (Secured) $_____ (Priority) $_____ (Total)

☐ Check this box if claim includes prepetition charges in addition to the principal amount of the claim. Attach itemized statement of all additional charges.

6. CREDITS AND SETOFFS: The amount of all payments on this claim has been credited and deducted for the purpose of making this proof of claim. In filing this claim, claimant has deducted all amounts that claimant owes to debtor.

7. SUPPORTING DOCUMENTS: Attach copies of supporting documents, such as promissory notes, purchase orders, invoices, itemized statements of running accounts, contracts, court judgments, or evidence of security interests. If the documents are not available, explain. If the documents are voluminous, attach a summary.

8. TIME-STAMPED COPY: To receive an acknowledgment of the filing of your claim, enclose a stamped, self-addressed envelope and copy of this proof of claim.

THIS SPACE IS FOR COURT USE ONLY

Date	Sign and print the name and title, if any, of the creditor or other person authorized to file this claim (attach copy of power of attorney, if any).

Penalty for presenting fraudulent claim: Fine of up to $500,000 or imprisonment for up to 5 years, or both. 18 U.S.C. §§152 and 3571.

PROOF OF CLAIM (Continued)

Richard Roe
123 Street Avenue
Anytown, XX, 01234
(555)-123-1234
Attorney for Secured Creditor:
ABC MORTGAGE CORPORATION

IN THE MATTER OF	: UNITED STATES BANKRUPTCY COURT
	: FOR THE DISTRICT OF _____
	:
	: Chapter 13
	: Case No. XX-XXXXX
JOHN DOE and MARY DOE, Debtors	:
	: PROOF OF SECURED CLAIM

---

    1. The undersigned who conducts business at 9999 Broadway, Anytown, XX, 01234, is Chief Loan Officer of ABC MORTGAGE CORPORATION, a corporation organized under the laws of the state of XXXXXXXXX, and is duly authorized to make this proof of claim on behalf of the secured creditor ABC MORTGAGE CORPORATION.

    2. The indebtedness owed and due to ABC MORTGAGE COMPANY, the claimant, at the time of the filing of the petition of Chapter 13 bankruptcy by JOHN DOE and MARY DOE, debtors, was in the sum of $100,100.10, together with lawful interest from November 1, 19XX, together with foreclosure legal fees and costs.

    3. The consideration for this debt is as follows: First Mortgage and Bond executed by the original mortgagor(s) and/or debtors JOHN DOE and MARY DOE on April 1, 19XX, in the original amount of $150,150.15, for premises commonly known as 99 Nineteenth Street, Sometown, XXXXXXXX.

    4. The writing upon which this claim is founded is attached hereto. Attached please find a copy of the bond and assignment.

    5. No judgment has been rendered on the claim.

    6. This claim is not subject to any setoff or counterclaim.

    7. No security interest is held for this claim except the aforesaid mortgage.

    8. THIS IS A SECURED CLAIM.

Signed _____
                Roger Moneycontrol,
                Chief Financial Officer
                ABC MORTGAGE CORPORATION

Dated: _____

NOTICE OF OBJECTION

Richard Roe
123 Street Avenue
Anytown, XX, 01234
(555)-123-1234
Attorney for Secured Creditor:
ABC MORTGAGE CORPORATION

IN THE MATTER OF	: UNITED STATES BANKRUPTCY COURT
	: FOR THE DISTRICT OF _____
	:
	: Chapter 13
	: Case No. XX-XXXXX
JOHN DOE and MARY DOE, Debtors	:
	: NOTICE OF OBJECTION

   The undersigned, attorney for Secured Creditor ABC MORTGAGE CORPORATION, the holder of a First Purchase Money Mortgage on the property of Debtors JOHN DOE AND MARY DOE at 99 Nineteenth Street, Sometown, XXXXXXX, hereby object to the confirmation of the Debtors' proposed Chapter 13 plan in the event that the Debtors fail to make the regular monthly mortgage payments to ABC MORTGAGE CORPORATION outside of the Chapter 13 Plan, in accordance with the provisions of said Plan, in violation of 11 U.S.C. § 1326.

   In the event the Debtors cure the aforesaid payments due outside the Chapter 13 Plan prior to the Confirmation Hearing, the undersigned will not appear at the Confirmation Hearing and the aforestated objection should be deemed waived.

Signed _____
              Richard Roe, Attorney for Secured
              Creditor, ABC MORTGAGE CORPORATION

Dated _____

LIEN CLAIM

W 973—Mechanic's Lien Claim. Revised 12/68.

JULIUS BLUMBERG, INC., LAW BLANK PUBLISHERS

IN THE OFFICE OF THE CLERK OF THE COUNTY OF

Claimant

vs.

LIEN CLAIM

Builder and

Owner

COUNTY OF **ss.:**

BE IT KNOWN, *that*

of the *of* *in the County of* claim a mechanic's lien upon the building and lands hereinafter described, pursuant to the provisions of the New Jersey Statutes 2A :44-64 to 2A :44-124 inclusive, as amended, for debt contracted and owing to the claimant , for labor performed and materials furnished for the erection and construction of said building of which claim the following are the details:

1. THE DESCRIPTION OF THE BUILDING and of the lot or curtilage upon which the lien is claimed, is as follows

The said building is

and the same is erected upon that lot of land or curtilage, situated in the *of* in the County of *and State of New Jersey,* described as follows:

LIEN CLAIM (Continued)

2. *THE NAME   OF THE OWNER   of the land and of the estate therein on which the lien is claimed,   as follows:*

who (or which) ha   an estate in fee simple therein

3. *THE NAME   OF THE PERSON   WHO CONTRACTED THE DEBT, and for whom, and at whose request the labor was performed and the materials furnished for which such lien is claimed, who   deemed the BUILDER   ,   as follows:*

4. *THE FOLLOWING IS A BILL OF PARTICULARS, exhibiting the amount and kind of labor performed and of materials furnished, and the prices at which and times when the same were performed and furnished, and giving credit for all the payments made thereupon and deductions that ought to be made therefrom, and exhibiting the balance justly due to such claimant   , to-wit:*

LIEN CLAIM (Continued)

All the above labor was performed and materials furnished between the   day

of   19   , and the   day of   19

which said last mentioned date is the date of the last work done and materials furnished for which said debt is due.

5. Claimant filed a Notice of Intention to furnish the labor and materials hereinbefore mentioned prior to the commencement of the work and prior to the commencement of deliveries of materials and gave notice in writing to the owner of the filing of said notice of intention, all in accordance with the said statute.

Dated:

L. S.

L. S.

L. S.

L. S.

LIEN CLAIM (Continued)

STATE OF NEW JERSEY,
COUNTY OF }*ss.:*

                                       of full age, being duly sworn on   *oath says that*
       is   *the*
claimant   named in the foregoing claim; that the bill of particulars and statements therein set forth
shown in said claim are true; that the same is for labor performed and materials furnished by the claimant
in the ERECTION   *of the building   in such claim described,*
at the times therein specified; and that the sum of
dollars and   *cents, being the amount as therein claimed, is justly due and owing to*
said claimant   from the said

and that   he has been duly authorized to make this proof on behalf of the claimant.

              Subscribed and sworn to before me
this   *day of* }
                            A. D. 19 }

COUNTY CLERK'S OFFICE

Claimant

against

Builder

Owner

Mechanic's Lien Claim

Attorney(s) for Claimant

No. ....

Summons was issued on the within lien
claim this................................day of
................................A. D. 19   , at the suit of
................................claimant, against
................................Builder and
................................Owner.

Clerk.

EXAMPLE OF NOTICE OF MOTION TO LIFT AUTOMATIC STAY

Richard Roe
123 Street Avenue
Anytown, XX, 01234
(555)-123-1234
Attorney for Secured Creditor:
ABC MORTGAGE CORPORATION

IN THE MATTER OF	:	UNITED STATES BANKRUPTCY COURT
	:	FOR THE DISTRICT OF _____
	:	
	:	Chapter 13
	:	Case No. XX-XXXXX
JOHN DOE and MARY DOE, Debtors	:	
	:	NOTICE OF MOTION TO LIFT
	:	AUTOMATIC STAY
TO: JOHN DOE	:	
99 NINETEENTH STREET	:	
SOMETOWN, XXXXXX	:	
	:	
MARY DOE	:	
99 NINETEENTH STREET	:	
SOMETOWN, XXXXXX	:	
	:	
ROBERT ROE, TRUSTEE	:	
100 CAPITOL STREET	:	
CAPITOL, XXXXXX	:	
	:	
JOSEPH JONES, ESQ.	:	
555 ATTORNEY BLVD.	:	
SOMETOWN, XXXXXX	:	

PLEASE TAKE NOTICE that on October 25, 19XX, at 10:30 a.m., or as soon as counsel may be heard, the undersigned, attorney for Secured Creditor ABC MORTGAGE CORPORATION, will move before the UNITED STATES BANKRUPTCY COURT, The Honorable Richard B. Richards presiding, for an Order Lifting the Automatic Stay with respect to the property of the Debtors, JOHN DOE and MARY DOE located at 99 Nineteenth Street, Sometown, XXXXXX, and allowing the Secured Creditor ABC MORTGAGE CORPORATION to continue its foreclosure action by reason of failure of the Debtors to make the regular monthly mortgage payments outside the Chapter 13 Plan.

Signed _____
Richard Roe, Attorney for Secured
Creditor ABC MORTGAGE CORPORATION

Dated _____

CERTIFICATION IN SUPPORT OF NOTICE OF MOTION
BY SECURED CREDITOR TO LIFT STAY

Richard Roe
123 Street Avenue
Anytown, XX, 01234
(555)-123-1234
Attorney for Secured Creditor:
ABC MORTGAGE CORPORATION

IN THE MATTER OF	: UNITED STATES BANKRUPTCY COURT
	: FOR THE DISTRICT OF _____
	:
	: Chapter 13
	: Case No. XX-XXXXX
JOHN DOE and MARY DOE, Debtors	:
	: CERTIFICATION IN SUPPORT OF NOTICE
	: OF MOTION TO LIFT STAY

ROGER MONEYCONTROL does hereby certify:

   1.   I am Chief Financial Officer of ABC MORTGAGE CORPORATION, acting on behalf of ABC MORTGAGE CORPORATION, the holder of a first Purchase Money Mortgage on the Debtors' property at 99 Nineteenth Street, Sometown, XXXXXXX, and I am the individual responsible for the handling of the books and records of aforesaid mortgage account, and I am fully aware of the contents thereof.

   2.   ABC MORTGAGE CORPORATION, the Secured Creditor, has not received a regular monthly payment on the aforesaid mortgage from the Debtor mortgagors since November 1, 19XX, through _____. The monthly mortgage payment due is $595.00 (five hundred ninety five dollars) and the late charge is $32.00 (thirty two dollars).

   3.   I make this Certification in Support of the Notice of Motion to Lift Automatic Stay.

   4.   Annexed hereto to this Certification are copies of the bond and mortgage assignment relating to the aforesaid premises, as well as a schedule indicating the total amount due on the mortgage account for aforesaid premises.

   5.   I hereby certify that the foregoing statements made by me are true. I am fully aware that if any of the foregoing statements made by me are wilfully false, I am subject to punishment.

Signed _____
Roger Moneycontrol, Chief Financial
Officer, ABC MORTGAGE CORPORATION

Dated _____

JUDGMENT LIFTING STAY

Richard Roe
123 Street Avenue
Anytown, XX, 01234
(555)-123-1234
Attorney for Secured Creditor:
ABC MORTGAGE CORPORATION

IN THE MATTER OF	: UNITED STATES BANKRUPTCY COURT
	: FOR THE DISTRICT OF _____
	:
	: Chapter 13
	: Case No. XX-XXXXX
JOHN DOE and MARY DOE, Debtors	:
	: JUDGMENT LIFTING STAY

This matter having been brought before the Court by Richard Roe, attorney for Secured Creditor ABC MORTGAGE CORPORATION, by Notice of Motion to Lift Automatic Stay, and it appearing that said Notice of Motion having been regularly served upon all concerned parties, and this Court noting that no responding papers to the Motion to Lift Automatic Stay having been filed with the officer of the Clerk of the Bankruptcy Court in accordance with Rule _____, and for good cause shown

IT IS ADJUDGED AND DECREED that the Stay pursuant to Section 362 of the Bankruptcy Code, covering real property at 99 Nineteenth Street, Sometown, XXXXXX, is hereby lifted.

JUDGMENT rendered this fifteenth day of December, 19XX.

Signed _____
　　　　　Richard B. Richards, Judge
　　　　　United States Bankruptcy Court
　　　　　for the District of _____

NOTICE OF APPEAL

DESIGNATION OF COURT

_____ DISTRICT OF _____

In re _____)
    [Set forth here all names including)
    married, maiden, and trade names used)
    by debtor within last 6 years])
)
) Case No. _____
                  Debtor)
) Chapter _____
Social Security No(s). _____ and all)
Employer's Tax Identification No(s). [if any])
    _____)

NOTICE OF APPEAL

_____, the plaintiff [or defendant or other party] appeals to the District Court [or the Bankruptcy Appellate Panel] from the final judgment [or order or decree (describe)] of the Bankruptcy Court entered in this adversary proceeding [or other proceeding (describe type)] on the _____ day of _____, 19_____.

    The parties to the judgment [or order or decree] appealed from and the names and addresses of their respective attorneys are as follows:

_____

_____

Dated: _____

                          _____
                                Attorney for Appellant

                          _____
                                      Address

INDEX